ART NOUVEAU JEWELRY

*A Practical Guide to Its History and Beauty,
with Pictures of Over 150 Pieces of Jewelry
and a Compendium of International Jewelers' Marks.*

by
Joseph Sataloff

DORRANCE & COMPANY, INCORPORATED
828 LANCASTER AVENUE • BRYN MAWR, PENNSYLVANIA 19010
Publishers Since 1920

Copyright © 1984 Joseph Sataloff
All Rights Reserved
ISBN 0-8059-2915-0
Library of Congress Catalog Card No. 83-91260
Printed in the United States of America
First Printing

To my dearest treasures,
Ruth, Bob, and Jody

CONTENTS

Preface   ix

Acknowledgments   xi

I. *Introduction to Art Nouveau*   1
Development of style. Characteristics. Relation to Victorian jewelry. Influence of Gothic, Renaissance, African, Rococo, Japanese, and other styles. Appearance in Architecture, literature, painting, sculpture, and especially the decorative arts. Origin in England and emergence in Paris and New York. The Poster Movement, Sarah Bernhardt, Grasset, Mucha. Samuel Bing, Paris Exposition.

II. *Introduction to Art Nouveau Jewelry*   5
Jewelry as providing best expression of Art Nouveau philosophy and style. Range of expression. Incorporation of multiple disciplines. Fantasy, sensuality. Innovative use of materials, line, color, and space. Description of Art Nouveau features and how to differentiate from Victorian and Art Deco styles. Use of horn, tortoise shell, glass. Acquisition of original masterpieces by Gulbenkian. Master jewelers in various countries. The genius of René Lalique. Other names for Art Nouveau style.

III. *The Beauty of Art Nouveau Jewelry*   8
Reasons for collecting antique jewelry—antiquity, rarity, intrinsic value, provenance, technique, etc. Unique attraction of Art Nouveau jewelry in design, color, innovative features, and emotional appeal. Comparison with masters of impressionistic painting. Rare combinations of color, especially in use of enamels. Exotic, mysterious, sensuous, suggestive, innovative. Plique à jour enameling. Motion. Transference of nature into works of art.

IV. *Types of Art Nouveau Jewelry* 10
Masterpieces for competitive exhibitions. Commissioned pieces. Monumental works in museums. Handcrafted work. Combinations of handwork and machine work. Larger numbers of stamped out silver and gold pieces for inexpensive markets. Unique pieces by Wolfers, Lalique, Fouquet.

V. *Enameling* 12
Advantages in color combinations, durability. Creative challenge. Plique à jour, plique à nuit, basse-taille, guilloche, cloisonné, champlevé, painted enamels, grissaille. Fabergé, Limoge, Thesmar, de La Croix.

VI. *Authenticating Art Nouveau Jewelry* 13
Quality. Design and composition. Materials and workmanship. Marks. Enameling. Appearance on the reverse. Sculpturing. Gemstones. Summary.

VII. *Silver Art Nouveau Jewelry* 17
Wide use for less expensive, mass-produced jewelry, especially in the United States. In England: Liberty & Co. style, influence of Arts and Crafts Movement, individuality of ideas and execution, machine and handmade, Cymric Style, enameled silver, Haseler of Birmingham, Murrle, Bennett & Co., Connell, Charles Horner. Germany: Fahrner. Austria. United States: Providence and Newark, Kerr & Co., Gorham, Unger Brothers.

VIII. *English Arts and Crafts Jewelry* 20
Reaction against mechanization. Search for ideas in Medieval and Renaissance art and life. John Ruskin. William Morris. Philosophy of movement. Limitations of excellence among Arts and Crafts jewelers. Formation of guilds and art schools. Leading figures: Ashbee, Birmingham, Artificers guild, Wilson, Cooper, Gaskin, Fisher, Dawson, Cuzner, Traquair, Liberty & Co., Knox. Materials and forms, enameling.

IX. *German Art Nouveau Jewelry* 23
Production of French style Art Nouveau jewelry. Pforzheim. Schmuckmuseam. Association with Paris. Jugendstil. Fahrner, Darmstadt designers, Zerrener, Fiessler, Riester, Kleeman, R. Koch. Austria: Roset and Fischmeister, Gurschner, Prutscher. Influence via Murrle, Bennett & Co.

X. *American Art Nouveau Jewelry* 27
Tiffany & Co. as foremost artistic jeweler in United States. Columbian Exposition, 1893. "Little Blue Book." New Tiffany style and materials. Louis C. Tiffany, influence on development of Art Nouveau style. Tiffany studios. Use of turquoise, demantoids, and other stones, scarabs and glass. St. Louis Exhibit, 1904. Artistic Art Jewelry. Ethnic influences. Competitors: Steuben and Marcus & Co. Julia Sherman at Tiffany's. Alling & Co., Bailey, Banks & Biddle, Kerr, Gorham, Unger Brothers, Arts and Crafts in Chicago, Koehler, Kalo, and others.

XI. *French Art Nouveau Jewelry*   33
Paris as nucleus of Art Nouveau. Gallé. Samuel Bing. Maison Moderne. Lalique and the development of French Art Nouveau Jewelry: technical skill, imagination, fantasy, enameling, philosophy of Art Nouveau, color, movement, ingenuity of design, carved glass, pâte de verre. Fouquet and Vever. Gaillard, Gautrait, and Descomps. Other important French jewelry makers.

XII. *Photographs and Captions*   39
Over 150 pieces of jewelry are pictured, most in color. Identifying captions point out important features of the jewelry and help demonstrate the difference between Art Nouveau jewelry and such styles as Art Deco and Victorian jewelry.

XIII. *International Jewelers and Marks Circa 1900*   65
Major listings: America, France, England. Other countries: Austria, Belgium, Denmark, Germany, Holland, Russia (including Fabergé workmasters), Spain and Portugal, Switzerland.

Bibliography   123

PREFACE

This book is filled with important information about Art Nouveau jewelry. Written from the viewpoint of a collector and dealer, it provides answers to most of the questions you will need to know in order to evaluate pieces of jewelry in the Art Nouveau style. It is based on extensive practical experience and research. It is not intended as a scholarly academic treatise or a critical, in-depth study of designers, techniques, or manufacturers of jewelry. Nevertheless, it is filled with basic information about the style and the period that will be of interest to dealers, collectors, and all persons who frequent antique shows or museum exhibits and love beautiful pieces of jewelry.

Emphasizing the practical problems involved in distinguishing authentic pieces of Art Nouveau jewelry, this book answers questions such as: What is Art Nouveau jewelry? How does it differ from pieces in the Victorian and Art Deco styles? Is a particular piece authentic Art Nouveau? Or, is it a reproduction or a revival piece? What aspects must be considered in evaluating each item? Is it handmade or machine made? Who designed and/or made it? Does it have a hallmark? What is the significance of the hallmark? Does the piece have quality?

Of particular importance to collectors and dealers is the list of more than 1,000 famous Circa 1900 French jewelers' marks included for the first time in any book, as well as hundreds of makers' names in America, England, Germany, and other countries. These marks and names will enable anyone to identify the maker of many pieces of jewelry whose origin currently may be considered "unknown." Also included are brief discussions of outstanding jewelers who designed and produced works in the Art Nouveau style. The comments accompanying each illustration often describe the beauty and singular features of the piece of jewelry and the characteristics of the goldsmith. Almost all the jewelry depicted is from private collections and has not been previously published.

ACKNOWLEDGMENTS

The author acknowledges the contributions made by scholars and authors such as Graham Hughes, Charlotte Gere, Shirley Bury, Dora Jane Jansen, and Betty Elzea. Through their writings and personal communications, they have contributed extensively to the contents of this book. Occasionally phrases are used that may have been extracted from the voluminous literature studied in preparing this book. A full bibliography is included to cover the references used and additional sources of information.

Special thanks is given to Irving Lewis whose superb taste was contagious and of inestimable influence on this author. The faculty and participants in the Annual Antique Jewelry Course at the University of Maine also made helpful contributions to the contents of this book. And to Gladys Koch the author extends particular credit for her assistance in providing a survey of Art Nouveau jewelry in the United States.

The following dealers, collectors and experts aided this publication: L. Ford, R. Esmerian, Kip Forbes, S. Klusner, Dora Jane Jansen, S. & M. Lewis, Dr. K. Hiesinger, J. Jonas, Fred Leighton, Dan Richter, Isi Fischzang, Andrew Nelson, E. Miles, David Callaghan, William Johnston, R. LaForet, I. Switt, Geoffrey Munn, Joanne Hardwick, Frances Fox Sandmel, Yvonne Brunhammer, Fred Brandt, and many others.

The author is most grateful to Vivienne Becker of London for her major contribution to this book. Her astute understanding and appreciation of Art Nouveau and her remarkable ability to articulate previously indescribable beauty have added luster and charm to this publication.

I appreciate the help from Ruth Giduck in the preparation of this manuscript.

With sincerest appreciation to Brian Shulik for producing such a beautiful and endearing book.

I

Introduction to Art Nouveau

Toward the end of the nineteenth century, an unusual artistic movement swept through Europe and America. Rising in France and England, and called by a variety of names such as *Art Nouveau, fin de siècle, Art Moderne,* and *Jugendstil,* the movement seemed suddenly to flow into being, startling the late Victorian art establishment with its new philosophy of freedom and uninhibited form. It turned its back on art conventions of the past, however much it may have naturally derived from them. Its emotional style, conveyed by a combination of gently curving lines, subtle and warm colors, and unique use of space and materials, appeared to be based on nothing that had been attempted before. Enthusiastically hailed as truly *nouveau,* or scorned with equal fervor, it flourished for about twenty years, and then suffered a sudden and unlamented demise. By about 1915, Art Nouveau was dead. Most obituary comments at the time expressed little regret at the passing of what has been described as a ludicrous and ephemeral artistic aberration.

For over fifty years, Art Nouveau languished in a kind of artistic limbo. As late as 1965 works by Beardsley, Mucha, Gallé, Tiffany, Lalique, Ashbee, and other giants of the time were unsought. Recently, however, the critical atmosphere has changed, and once more the spirit of Art Nouveau pervades the consciousness of our society. Although returning as "Art Déjà Vu," the impact of the style has had the same reception that it had originally, and it has established itself as a serious movement permeating many forms of art.

The Art Nouveau style was a radical change from the somberness, sentimentality, and strict adherence to defined rules that characterized English and French artistic expression in the 1860s and 1870s. It developed in response to the emotional needs of the times, emerging from the bonds of Victorian traditionalism. It is interesting that the freedom and emotional release expressed by Art Nouveau cannot survive in a restrictive environment. Though it rose, and now thrives, in western Europe and has been received by the United States, Fabergé's attempt to introduce and establish Art Nouveau in Russia met with only superficial success. The daring independence of its lyric, airy design was so new and distinctive that it acquired from its most ardent proponent, Samuel Bing in Paris, the lasting name, "New Art." Bing envisioned all decorative arts as linking man to his environment, and proposed that the new style be applied to painting, sculpture, furniture, jewelry, weaving, and even wallpaper. Salons opened in Paris to exhibit works illustrative of the new movement.

The roots of Art Nouveau design lie in a number of different areas. The designers of the period extracted elements from other ages and from other lands. Each artist took features of design from previous ages and combined, used, or reinterpreted them in a unique, personal way to produce a revolutionary new style. In Celtic manuscript pages, brooches, and chalices they found intricate linear designs of tangled interlaces and coiled spirals. From Gothic art they extracted certain aspects of its mysterious flamelike and leaflike tracery, its double-curved ogee arches and flowing shapes. Other inspiration came from the art imported from Java, Africa, and other exotic lands. The Art Nouveau style may also be considered a natural outgrowth of the Rococo style of the previous period that was distinguished by its flowing space, asymmetrical ornamentation, and vigorous curves.

Japanese art, particularly the two-dimensional planar aspects; its broad homogeneous, receding planes; "the evocative quality of the line in establishing a linear rhythm; the expressive contours; the use of color for flat pattern effect instead of illusionistic modeling;" and its simplification of natural form also had a tremendous impact on the arts and designers of the period.

The late nineteenth century was a time of boldness, a time in which people were eager for new ideas. It was a period of colonial expansion, and products from exotic lands flooded the European marketplace. It was also a period that produced bold styles in writing, music, painting, architecture, and especially the decorative arts.

This was the age that witnessed the publication of novels such as Stephen Crane's *Maggie: A Girl of the Streets*, and Thomas Hardy's *Tess of the D'Urbervilles* and *Jude the Obscure*, which presented social, political, and religious issues through the actions of the characters themselves. It was the era of such poets as Kipling and Yeats and the playwrights Oscar Wilde, Ibsen, and Chekhov.

The music world was astir with composers who were attempting to work out new concepts of tonality and to reconcile with new harmonic idioms the other musical elements of instrumentation, counterpoint, rhythm, and form. The great composers—Dvořák, Puccini, Mahler, Debussy, Richard Strauss, and others—were all striving for new expression of their art. Stephen Foster and Charles Ives incorporated many folk elements into their compositions that achieved great popularity in the United States.

The United States suddenly leaped ahead in its architectural design. Frank Lloyd Wright had begun to design structures in his unique "prairie style" and early "skyscrapers" were springing up in the major cities. Although Art Nouveau had a limited influence on this architecture, still certain of its characteristics are evident in the decorative detail on some of the buildings of the period. A splendid example is Louis Henry Sullivan's use of ornament on the Carson-Pirie-Scott Building in Chicago. In handsome cast-iron detail, Sullivan decorated the lower two stories of this building with a curious and personal combination of leaves, flowers, geometric motifs, classical ornament, and typical Art Nouveau elements.

The intellectual world was astir with the late writing of Nietzsche and with William James's *Principles of Psychology* and *The Will to Believe and Other Essays*. Sociology was just beginning to emerge: Émile Durkheim published *Le Suicide* in 1897, the first truly scientific sociological study.

Important technological advances brought about many new inventions to add to the length and enjoyment of human life. Wilhelm Roentgen's discovery of the X ray provided the medical community with a diagnostic tool of incredible importance. Guglielmo Marconi's wireless was to have a tremendous impact on the world both in communications and entertainment. More and more use was being found for electricity, and inventors were working on the diesel engine, gas-powered motors, submarines, and motion pictures.

It is not too surprising, therefore, that the decorative arts were also experiencing dramatic changes. Some of these early stirrings are seen in the Arts and Crafts movement begun in the 1850s in England by the designer William Morris. Morris favored the applied arts and believed that rooms should be designed *en suite*, from furniture, wallpaper, and fabrics to details such as door handles. Morris's work was not truly Art Nouveau, but many of his ideas provided inspiration for other great Art Nouveau designers who strived to find a unity of expression in their design.

Although the new movement may have begun in England, it was in Paris that Art Nouveau emerged in all its glory in the 1890s. At this time in history Paris was a city devoted to pleasure, and the citizens gave full rein to its pursuit. They were flamboyant, they were exuberant, and they were eagerly looking for the new and the exciting. It was only natural that they quickly adopted the new look in decorative arts that exploded in Paris and subsequently spread throughout the Continent and to the United States.

Art Nouveau design was interpreted in slightly different ways in each country. In France, for example, the style was airy, imaginative, free, and delightful. In England, because of the Arts and Crafts movement, there was much more emphasis on craft than on artistic expression. Objects produced in England were usually made of silver rather than gold, and brightly colored rather than pastel enamels were used. Blister pearls, moonstone, and lacy goldwork predominated, and the natural forms of the French Art Nouveau were not found. In Belgium, the designers used an interpretation that was similar to that of the French jewelers. The style of the period was called Jugendstil in Germany, and the unique interpretation of the German artists may be seen in jewelry. Portuguese artists had some stylistic differences, but for the most part their work was similar to that of the French. The American firms of Tiffany and Marcus & Company also interpreted Art Nouveau in their own distinctive fashions.

Artists of the day were primarily concerned with the idea behind the work rather than the work itself.

Like the poets who tended to dissociate their verses from established patterns and to seek more untamed expression of ideas and sensations, the artists wished to present their ideas through the use of symbols that appealed to the emotions rather than to the intellect. They tended to feel that the symbol was both the key to the meaning and the meaning itself.

Among the artists of the period, Gauguin and Edvard Munch stand out as individuals who expressed their ideas by means of evocative and decorative form. The drawings of Aubrey Beardsley, with their wide, sweeping lines and flat background, had a tremendous effect on the popularity of the poster movement, which, in turn, contributed to the growing popularity of Art Nouveau. The importance of the poster movement, especially in France, is evidenced by the poster exhibition inaugurated in 1894 and by the extensive coverage of the works of poster artists in periodicals. The symbolist magazine *La Plume*, in fact, devoted an entire issue to the works of Eugène Grasset.

Sarah Bernhardt was the subject of many popular posters of the period. Grasset had created a poster for Bernhardt's *Jeanne d'Arc*, but she was unhappy with it because it stresses the medieval atmosphere of the play rather than her personal attributes. Later that year, Madame Bernhardt engaged Alphonse Mucha to design a poster for her new production of *Ghismonda*. She was so pleased with this poster that Mucha was placed under contract to her for a number of years. Mucha used areas of flat color enclosed in strong lines, but in a much less restrained manner than did Grasset, and he highlighted her long flowing hair in fantastic patterns. Bernhardt also wore many fabulous pieces of jewelry designed in the Art Nouveau style and her enormous popularity had an important effect in advancing both the poster movement and the Art Nouveau movement itself.

Toulouse-Lautrec, of course, is especially noted for his posters. The dancers and entertainers of the Montmartre district of Paris were his most popular subjects. His posters depict these persons with such evil elegance and with a personal vision at once ruthless and factual.

Other poster artists of the time include Steinlen, Moreau-Nelaton, de Feure, Orazi, and Bonnard.

French architects included aspects of Art Nouveau design in their structures. The energetically flowing, tensely coiling line charged with power and force is evident in the structures erected throughout Paris by Guimard, Horta, and van de Velde. Guimard's powerfully expressive cast-iron orchid-like stalks still stand at the entrance to several Paris metro stations. Elements of Art Nouveau design were also incorporated in pieces of furniture designed by persons such as Émile Gallé, Victor Prouvé, Louis Majorelle, and Hector Guimard.

Art Nouveau design, however, reached its zenith in jewelry making. The purpose and scale of items of jewelry gave vent to the artists' use of intricate and capricious play of lines. They used plant and insect motifs with a great degree of freedom, creating unique miniature sculptures that were a delight to behold. They also chose materials with great thought regarding the subtlety of colors, which heightened the symbolic imagery the artists wished to convey.

An early forerunner of Art Nouveau jewelry was a bracelet by Froment-Meurice which was shown at the 1851 Great Exhibition in London. This piece incorporated silver angels divided by panels of enameled ivy leaf tracery. Froment-Meurice drew inspiration from the legends of the Gothic era and the Renaissance tales of knights and maidens in distress. His firm produced many pieces in the Art Nouveau style and his important contribution to jeweler's art is summed up in his obituary published in *Le Siècle:* "No one has ever demonstrated so clearly that art had a right to a place in every sphere. Particularly in his jewelry, so simple in appearance, he showed an inventiveness, a delicacy and a gracefulness of execution which had been long forgotten."

The term "Art Nouveau" was first applied to the movement with the opening in December 1895 of Samuel Bing's *La maison de l'art nouveau*. Bing commissioned Bonnard, Grasset, Ibels, Sérusier, Toulouse-Lautrec, Ranson, Vuillard, and others to make designs for stained glass pieces. In addition, he introduced paintings by these artists, sculpture by Rodin, glass by Gallé and Tiffany, jewelry by Lalique, and the posters by Beardsley, Bradley, and Mackintosh.

"Art Nouveau Bing" was a special pavilion at the Paris Exposition Universelle of 1900 and as such was an important attraction. Firms from the United States attending this exposition were intrigued by this exhibit and returned home to introduce the style to their customers. However, this exhibition proved to be both the zenith and the finale of Art

Nouveau. The new design, that at once shocked and delighted the world, went into swift decline. It simply became too popular and its mass production caused it to go out of vogue.

Art Nouveau remained a viable style in jewelry longer than in other art forms. However by 1915, most designers and jewelry makers were no longer producing pieces typical of true Art Nouveau.

II
Introduction to Art Nouveau Jewelry

Although Art Nouveau design appeared in virtually every aspect of the decorative arts—from massive bedroom chests to advertising posters—fine pieces of jewelry of the period provide the best examples of what Art Nouveau was all about.

The distinctive features of Art Nouveau were most vividly evident in the artistic jewelry of the period; more than any other medium, jewelry seemed to lend itself to the very essence of Art Nouveau. It permitted a wide variety of shapes, forms, materials, and it incorporated goldwork, sculpture, painting, enameling, and gem setting into its range of expression. Furthermore, jewelry has always been made to be pleasing, and, turned to this purpose, the romantic inventiveness of the new style could be given its full scope.

Jewelry was one of the purest and most apt expressions of the Art Nouveau movement. Jewel design was overdue for an injection of fresh talent after the nineteenth century derivative parade of patterns, stale ideas, excessive sentimentality, and for the most part, the absence of any artistic element. Art jewelers like Carlo Giuliano and brilliant goldsmiths like Castellani had brightened the Victorian outlook, but all had drawn on the past for inspiration.

Mechanization and the mass markets had further debased design and manufacture.

The instigators of Art Nouveau seized on this ailing art form and exploited the age-old element of fantasy and magic in jewels. Also, they saw that the traditions of gems and intrinsic values and skills were begging to be turned upside down. Their symbols, themes, and messages fitted the purpose of feminine adornment and its implicit sensuality long buried in Victorian priggishness. Craftsmen found that the restrictions imposed by jewel design were minimal, and were pushed ever further to their outermost limits by jewelers like Lalique. This meant of course that sometimes the jewels were unwearable, impractical exhibition pieces, but fantastic and beautiful works of art.

Art Nouveau was short-lived but forceful as an art movement. A product of many fermenting social and artistic factors, it burst through with a zest and intensity that was sometimes overpowering. But like any revolution it had to be forceful and extreme to make an impact and achieve its aims. Applied to jewelry, all the elements, skills, and emotions came together successfully.

The lines of Art Nouveau jewelry were curved and free, portraying a sense of organic motion. Flowers seemed to be moving and twisting; birds and insects, flying. Art Nouveau was never passive, always flowing, in harmony with nature, and consonant with the temperament of the connoisseurs and sophisticates of the 1890s. The colors of the jewelry were soft and warm: tawny orange, silvers, and grays, along with lemon yellow, pearly white, and flesh. Pastel colors blended into one another with a subtleness and delicacy that challenges description.

Such colors and graceful curving lines were in marked contrast to the Art Deco style that followed soon after. Intense color, bold combinations, and concise, well-defined lines in geometrical patterns were certain indications of Art Deco. In Art Deco jewelry, great importance was placed on the complimentary colors of stones set in a single piece. Stones previously of little value were used tirelessly throughout the period. Red orange coral was used with deep blue lapis lazuli and apple green jade. Black and white onyx and brilliant diamonds were used with startling and abrupt effect. But Art Nouveau, continuously bending in modulations of a circle, made no use of abruptness or angles. It is this shunning of angles and sharp lines, and the spirit of the free-flowing emotion it reflects, to which psychedelic art finds itself in sympathy, if not indebted. Amaya, who wrote a definitive monograph on Art Nouveau some fifty years after its inception, says of it, "It continues to fascinate, with its fantasy of invention, its predictions of mid twentieth century functionalism and its touching desire to unify all elements of life into a perfectly ordered new world of social reform."

Again, jewelry can be taken to exemplify the movement as a whole. A good piece of jewelry may appear to be only decorative, but it is alive with emotion; the more one looks at it the more its beauty is perceived and felt. The fine pieces of the period might be described by the comment made of Beethoven's music, "From the heart it has sprung, and to the heart it will penetrate." Quite apart from the cheap imitations that have inevitably proliferated around it (the sensuous, overdrawn females with flowing hair or twisting snakes; the long-stemmed, sinuous glasses; or many-colored lampshades with dripping edges), Art Nouveau has produced the most imaginative and original jeweled master pieces in history. The urge for expression, instinct, in the new form materialized in bold applications of color and uses of materials rarely seen before in jewelry: horn, tortoise shell, and notably the exquisitely ephemeral-looking enamel, especially *plique à jour*.

The most artistic pieces of this jewelry were quickly acquired by sophisticated collectors like Gulbenkian, Walters, Citroen, and Esmerian, and museums such as Le Musée des Artes Decoratif in Paris. The jewelry that has reached the general public has frequently consisted of cheaper castings and inferior reproductions, an unfortunate contrast which has given rise to some short-sighted deprecation of the style at its best.

While artists in many countries contributed much to Art Nouveau it was the French jewelers such as Lalique, Fouquet, Vever, Gaillard and Gautrait whose efforts raised jewelry from a minor to a major art form. In England, Ashbee, Wilson, and Murphy; Wolfers in Belgium; Masriera in Portugal; Koch in Germany; and Tiffany in America also made important contributions. The creator of Art Nouveau jewelry, however, was René Lalique. Though he is most famous for his work in glass, he was the greatest master jeweler of his time. In the late nineteenth century, it was he who revolutionized the jewelers' art.

Lalique viewed jewelry making not as a craft traditionally devoted to emphasizing precious stones and costly metals of high intrinsic value, but as an opportunity for creating an object of art no less serious than a painting or a sculpture. Costliness of material became incidental. Rather, his jeweled works were often designed specifically to fit the personality of the wearer, an astonishing approach for a jeweler of his time. More than anyone else, he merits the praise implicit in Graham Hughes's descriptive analysis made some fifty years after his day: "It has been said that the best jewelers are those who understand people as well as technique; who want to flatter the wearer as well as extend the art. Given free play artistically, most artists will enjoy jewelry, and it is the quality of abandon expressed in shapes which may turn a vague conception into a beautiful jewel. The best jewels are the most imaginative, the most unique and the most diverse in inspiration."

René Lalique was indisputably a creative genius and a leader of the Art Nouveau movement. The fact that he originally applied his talents to jewelry lends more emphasis to the jewel as a work of art at this period. Lalique trained to the highest technical standards and perfected his skills before turning away from all set concepts of jewel composition. He drew inspiration from nature, from his childhood's unsentimental observations of the natural world, introducing a startling dreamlike quality into his creations. Insects, for example, long a favorite motif for young ladies' genteel brooches, suddenly transformed into shocking fantasy creatures; the innocuous butterfly was changed to a dragonfly with wings so real that they threatened to flap uncomfortably, and it grinned with a nightmarish mask that turned out to be, on closer examination, a young girl's face. Flowers once preserved in jewel form only in the most immaculate bloom, now looked tired, overblown, symbolically decaying at the edges, and suggested the cycle of birth, death, and rebirth. The unmentionable female form emerged, unclothed, hair unloosed, struggling towards freedom. A new kind of beauty, a surging sensuality, and free-flowing movement were unleashed with the strength of long repression. Together with these high ideals came a new concern for quality of life, for art in everyday living, and for a pride of performance and workmanship that helped Art Nouveau jewels stand the test of time.

Not only did Lalique design his own jeweled works of art, but he often did his own goldwork, enameling, gem setting, sculpturing, and engraving. He created a harmony of color, material, and form that was unique to jewelry. But decoration through the manipulation of materials, the traditional purpose of jewelry, was not his chief objective. His aim was expression. His emphasis was on the spiritual, the emotional and the mystical, the subtle and imaginative. He applied these qualities to what his mind's eye observed in nature and portrayed them in his creations. What he had to say he said in the simplest manner without redundancy, and he did so with a sensuous delight that entrances the observer. The artist transcends sheer intellectuality and provides the emotional fulfillment that alone can satisfy man. Entrancing as they were in Lalique's day, his pieces were criticized by some as being too heroic to be wearable. At the same time, however, the master created many smaller pieces for less spectacular adornment, in which he achieved a degree of perfection in precise detail that was the envy of his fellow craftsmen. The secret of these fine details lay in Lalique's use of a reduction machine. Applying a method used hitherto generally in medal making—and still predominantly so employed today—Lalique started out by making large models on which the master could produce the desired effects by means of conventional tools; then the reduction machine reproduced these details in a tiny jewel with absolute perfection.

Ivory had long been used in ornamentation, but it remained for Lalique to introduce the use of horn. A special horn was not available for the jewelry trade, and Lalique had to pick up his raw material at the Paris stockyards. Previously the master had kept an especially beautiful piece of horn on his writing desk; then suddenly the idea came to him to use it in a bracelet. He recognized the material's translucency and the charm with which it could be carved and ornamented with silver appliqué. Encouraged by his first effort, the artist soon combined horn, ivory, enamels, and gold in combs of exquisite beauty.

However, it was not merely the surprising use of new materials that distinguished Lalique's artistry. He excelled because of the exuberant scope of his vision, the elegance of his line, and the refinement of his finished work.

The style of design known today as Art Nouveau was called by many other names in its heyday. In France, it was referred to as *Style nouille,* (noodle style) *Modern Style, Style de bouche de Metro,* and even as *Style Guimard,* for Hector Guimard, the man responsible for the ornate subway entrances erected during that period. In Germany, it was frequently known as *Belgische* and *Veldesche,* after Henry van de Velde, as well as *Schnörkelstil* (flourish style) and *Bandwurmstil* (tapeworm style) and *Jugendstil,* from the Munich magazine *Jugend* (youth).

To Austrians, it was *Secessions-stil* because of the Vienna Secession which held highly cosmopolitan exhibitions. In England, it was sometimes referred to as *Studio-Stil,* after the publications which reflected the work of the Arts and Crafts Exhibition Society. In Belgium, it was *Paling style* (eel style) or *Le Style des Vingt* or *La Libre Esthêtique* (exhibition groups). To Italians, it was *Stile floreale* and *Stile Liberty,* after Liberty's of London store. In Scotland, it was the *Glasgow School,* and in Spain, *Modernismo.*

No matter what it was called, it was a design that blossomed throughout the western world for a brief spell. Many pieces of jewelry were produced during that time. Some were great masterpieces, others fine jewelry, and many merely interesting collector's items. This text will tell you about Art Nouveau jewelry, the famous designers of the period and the techniques they used. Most importantly, it provides guidelines you can use to evaluate Art Nouveau jewelry. It shows you how to assess both craftsmanship and design, and it includes numerous photographs of jewelry you may use as standards of comparison.

III

The Beauty of Art Nouveau Jewelry

Antique jewelry has fascinated collectors throughout the ages for a variety of reasons. Some items are collected because they are old, and their value comes from their antiquity. Other pieces portray the tastes and customs of past generations, such as Egyptian, Greek, or Roman cultures. Still others exemplify certain techniques, such as gold granulations, *plique à jour* enameling, etc., or superb craftsmanship, apparent in the works of Fabergé, Guiliano, and Castalani. All pieces of antique jewelry have beauty and value for particular reasons, but it is the jewelry of the Art Nouveau style that has emotional appeal plus all of the above.

What is it about Art Nouveau jewelry that touches the hearts of sophisticated and critical collectors? The breathtaking beauty of its style is the simple, yet obvious, answer. Art Nouveau is not a style that provides the showcase for magnificent precious stones, nor is it one that merely produces pretty little baubles. Instead, it is a philosophy that permits artists to give full rein to their creative talents, and the works of art they have created exhibit a beauty that evokes an emotional response unmatched in any other style.

The beauty found in the finest pieces of Art Nouveau jewelry may be likened to that found in the paintings of Renoir, Seurat, or Gauguin. Such pieces are truly works of art, masterpieces of design. They are not merely items of adornment, but are pieces that move the beholder because of a distinctive quality that goes much deeper than merely being pretty. Fine pieces are expressive; they are always pleasing. The design is never filled with turmoil, conflict, or other disruptive elements; it conveys harmony, beauty, and peace.

Among the attributes of Art Nouveau jewelry that make it so emotionally beautiful are: subtle color and shading, suggestion of form, delicate turns, and mystical imagery. Such aspects of Art Nouveau pieces evoke a sense of excitement. The more one views them, the deeper and more meaningful becomes their intrinsic beauty. They are imaginative pieces, daring and different from other styles and forms.

The exquisite beauty of the jewelry comes not from spectacular stones set in precious metals, as had previously been the case, but from the overall design and composition of individual pieces, each of which conveys a beauty that is often inexplicable. Its loveliness defies description because the design itself seems to render a sense of the exotic or the mysterious that leaves the viewer with a sense of wonder. The good pieces are so dramatic that, in many ways, they can be likened to a still shot from a motion picture that freezes a moment in time. In most of the jewelry items, the artist depicts a special moment he has captured, and the observer can only guess what has preceded it or what is to follow. The viewer cannot always sense what was in the mind of the artist who created the piece, and the sense of mystery is an important aspect of Art Nouveau. The human female, frequently unclothed and seemingly caught in a struggle to escape upwards, was another subject used extensively in the design. The artists like to depict the head of a lovely girl with her hair swirling about her and a semi-erotic or wistful, dreamy expression on her face. The peacock with its iridescent feathers and proud display of colors was used extensively in Art Nouveau design.

Plique à jour enameling was probably the single most important technique used by Art Nouveau designers in making their jewelry so appealing. In this style of enameling, transparent enamels are fused into the openings of a metal filigree in a manner that produces an effect suggestive of stained glass. *Plique à jour* and other subtle shading and color combinations, never before utilized in jewelry design, gave to Art Nouveau jewelry a distinctive appearance much like a three-dimensional painting. They created miniature sculptures in gold and silver. They created artistic masterpieces of incredible beauty.

Many other innovative features contributed to making good Art Nouveau design unique. Design in fine pieces is rarely static; it portrays motion as well as emotion. For example, the swallows by Lalique (Figure 49) are poised in flight and one can practically feel the wind blowing. Such a concept in jewelry design was indeed unique. Designers of the period cast aside inhibitions and conventions and brought a new boldness and innovation to their designs. Nature was also most prevalent in the design of Art Nouveau jewelry. The designers of the period took a firsthand look at nature and transferred the more exotic aspects of it—orchids, lilies, irises, ferns, snakes, dragonflies, peacocks, swans, etc.—to most of their creations. Trees, flowers, and other forms extended beyond the borders of the pieces; lines reached into space giving free rein to the imagination. Remarkable perspective was attained with sculptured and colored golds (Figure 3) and with enamels (Figure 24). Art Nouveau jewelry has yet to receive full measure of critical investigation for its aesthetic and technical aspects. The old adage "Beauty is in the eyes of the beholder" is certainly true, and the beholder of pieces of Art Nouveau jewelry can never deny its intrinsic beauty.

IV
Types of Art Nouveau Jewelry

Art Nouveau jewelry was made for individuals and for exhibitions and competitions. Its size ranged from monumental pieces, too large to be worn, to small exquisite creations. There were thousands of jewelers in America and Europe during the Art Nouveau period. Most of these firms had been producing jewelry that emphasized precious and semiprecious stones. With the introduction of the Art Nouveau style by jewelers such as Lalique, Tiffany, Liberty, and Bing, a veritable revolution took place within the industry and many jewelers quickly adopted the new style. Some became completely enthralled with it and produced jeweled masterpieces especially for exhibitions and competitions. Some of these pieces are monumental, being more than one foot in length and completely unwearable. Critics, of course, attacked these huge pieces, complaining that they were too heroic to be considered jewelry.

Fortunately there was one place where large, gaudy jewelry was needed—the stage. Among the actresses who clamored for Lalique's heroic designs was Sarah Bernhardt, the "toast of France." For her Lalique designed magnificent headdresses, belts, necklaces, etc., which she wore for her role in *Theodora*. These pieces could be easily seen by the audience. Lalique also designed similar spectacular ornaments for Mme. Bartet which she wore in her role of *Bernice*. The beauty of these stage jewels became the talk of Paris, and thus the Art Nouveau style was authoritatively sponsored and effectively displayed.

Many of these monumental jewels, especially those made by Lalique, were subsequently purchased by the very wealthy C. Gulbenkian and now can be found in the Gulbenkian Museum in Portugal. Others have been acquired by other museums and only rarely does one find any of these large pieces on the market. When they do appear, they are extremely expensive. These truly monumental works may be studied in a fashion similar to the imperial eggs by Fabergé in the Forbes Museum in New York or the remarkable jewels by Dali now in the Richmond Museum in Virginia.

For the most part, however, the Art Nouveau jewelers made small pieces of jewelry. Some of these were made for exhibition purposes and are now considered masterpieces. These pieces can be worn, but basically they were produced as works of art to demonstrate the designer's skill in goldwork, enameling, design, painting, or sculpturing. Most of the illustrations in this book represent this particular group of Art Nouveau jewelry. Important features of each piece are noted in the captions that accompany the photographs. Many of these pieces were made by hand, either totally or in part, and as such they are miniature works of art—three-dimensional jeweled masterpieces. Pieces such as these become available to collectors from time to time either through auctions, dealers, or private collectors.

Of lesser importance, but still indicative of the Art Nouveau style, were pieces made solely for female adornment. Some of these pieces were expensive and others relatively inexpensive. Some were exact copies of very fine pieces, but were produced by machine or by a combination of machine and hand. Many other Art Nouveau pieces were modifications of important and particularly fine pieces of jewelry; however, they too were at least partially machine produced. All of these pieces are very worthwhile from a collector's standpoint. Frequently they can be found in antique shops and at shows and auctions. The pieces enameled in the *plique à jour* style are particularly important. Also, pieces of the period that are stamped with the maker's name, and those that are gold (many of which were copied from original handmade pieces), are valuable collector's items.

Large numbers of silver Art Nouveau pieces were also produced in varying sizes during the period. These include large buckles, brooches, hair combs, and so forth. The firms of Unger Brothers and Kerr in the United States were large producers of silver Art Nouveau jewelry. These firms also made copies of other jewelry designed in the British Arts and Crafts style. Signed pieces of both of these styles of jewelry are worthwhile additions to any collection. Due to a resurgence of interest in the Art Nouveau period, however, many reproductions are currently being produced and marketed. The collector must beware, because these are not valuable collectables in the same sense as pieces reproduced during the period.

Practically all of the jewelers producing pieces in the Art Nouveau style made a certain number of less expensive items for everyday wear. Even great masters goldsmiths like Lalique created many pieces for ordinary feminine adornment, as well as accessories for men such as watch fobs, rings, key chains, stick pins. Even in these pieces, Lalique achieved a great degree of perfection and precision of detail that was the envy of his fellow craftsmen. The secret of these fine details lay in Lalique's use of his reduction machine.

Outstanding pieces of Art Nouveau jewelry are so unusual in today's commercial market that one is inclined to think that all such pieces are unique and were made solely by artists like Lalique, Fouquet, or Gautrait. Actually, very few of even the most elaborate and monumental pieces are unique and made entirely by a single artist. Undoubtedly Lalique, Fouquet, Wolfers, and other designers were capable of doing their own get setting, sculpturing, enameling, designing, etc., and in fact probably did produce some of their early pieces entirely by themselves. But, in general, a designer created the concept and made his drawings much like an architect might do, while other workers in the firm made their own special contributions to the finished item. For instance, Lalique and Mucha were outstanding and imaginative designers. Feuillâtre and Thesmar were extraordinary enamelists. Vernon was an exceptional medalist and engraver. Each large firm had numerous workmen who contributed to the production of its jewelry. Much time and expense were involved in creating these pieces of art, and consequently were quite expensive and could be purchased only by the wealthy or by museums. Such unique pieces rarely filter down to the average buyer of jewelry. Unfortunately, this is not a very democratic aspect of Art Nouveau.

A number of master goldsmiths did indeed make unique pieces. Philippe Wolfers, for example, made a substantial number of unique items which bear the stamp *"exemplair unique."* Lalique and Fouquet also made a number of unique pieces, but these were done primarily on commission or for exhibition purposes. The pieces on exhibit at the Gulbenkian Museum provide an excellent source for investigating and evaluating the workmanship, style, and quality of the individual arts and of outstanding Art Nouveau jewelry.

V

Enameling

The use of color enamels developed by Art Nouveau jewelers made a major contribution to art in general and, in particular, served to bridge the gap between art and craft. By using shaded enamels that changed imperceptibly according to the light and angle from which the piece was viewed, and by combining these enamels with gold wires to establish perspective, the artists of the period were able to make pieces of jewelry that matched the sheer delight and beauty previously evoked only in paintings.

Enamels had been used to decorate jewelry for hundreds of years, but not in the unique fashion used by the Art Nouveau designer. Enamels do not tarnish, they can be made in endless subtle variations of colors, and they are resistant to wear. All previous metals can be enameled successfully, with the possible exception of platinum.

There are many methods of applying enamels. Those methods primarily used by the Art Nouveau jewelers involved transparent and opaque enamels. In transparent enameling, the enamel is generally thin and one can see through it. It may be as clear as glass or it may be colored. When the enamel has no metal backing, such as gold or silver, and it can be seen through, it is called *plique à jour*. This is a very difficult technique to master, one which requires removing the metal backing after firing and retaining the enamel cloisons in a gold reticulum. *Plique à jour* technique was extremely popular with the Art Nouveau jewelers because its successful use was further evidence of their skill and artistry. When transparent enamel is applied to the surface of a metal placque it is called *plique à nuit*. In *plique à nuit*, one can still see through the enamel to the surface of the metal placque on which designs may be engraved. Remarkable light effects are obtained with this method and it was a favorite technique of Fabergé. By careful use of engraving tools and by working in light relief, different types of chromatic intensity were obtained, as in *basse-taille* and *guilloches*.

Both transparent and opaque enamels were applied to metals using a variety of methods. In *cloisonné*, the enamel is placed in compartments *(cloisons)* made by thin wires or strips. Russian and Chinese enamel objects are outstanding examples of *cloisonné* work. *Champlevé* enameling involves a technique in which channels and compartments are carved into a piece of metal and then filled with enamel, leaving a comparatively smooth surface of enamel and metal. Limoge enameling is a good example of *champlevé* and also of painting with enamels *(émail peinture)*. Opaque enamels generally were used for this technique. A subspecialty of this method is called *grisaille*. In *grisaille*, white figures are used on a dark background. In the *basse-taille* method *(basse* means low; *taille*, cut), the subject is carved in low relief beneath the general surface of the metal so that after enameling, the surface is entirely smooth and the relief is seen through the transparent enamel.

Art Nouveau jewelers utilized all of these enameling methods and sometimes they incorporated several of them in the design of a single piece of jewelry. The distinguished enamelist Thesmar enlarged the size of the enameled *plique à jour* cloisons as early as 1878 and shaded the enamels in each section. Suau de la Croix developed a singular type of *plique à jour* enamel with thick curved glass cloison that resembled stained glass but simulated gemstones such as emeralds, rubies, and amethysts. He worked mostly with silver and combined real gemstones with enamels and carved ivory to produce bright colored jewelry of remarkable style.

VI
Authenticating Art Nouveau Jewelry

An experienced collector of Art Nouveau jewelry relates an experience he had in authenticating Art Nouveau pieces which is typical of what may happen to collectors:

> My first problem in authenticating Art Nouveau jewelry occurred in 1975 when a dealer offered me eight beautiful pieces in the Art Nouveau style. Some of these were enameled, some were *plique à jour,* and all were stamped "Cashriera," a maker of particularly fine antique jewelry in Portugal in the 1900s. However, there was something very strange about the pieces: they all looked brand new. Having previously encountered a smiliar experience with ten flowers signed "Fabergé," all of which proved to have been made recently in New York, I was naturally suspicious. Careful examination of these "Cashriera" pieces confirmed my initial impression that these were pieces recently made in the Art Nouveau style. They were not authentic; to be more exact, they were "revival pieces." They were being misrepresented as pieces "of the period."

It is easy to be misled, particularly when pieces are well made and attractive. It is therefore necessary to consider the factors that are important in authenticating and evaluating Art Nouveau jewelry.

Quality

Quality is the first thing to consider in assessing a piece of Art Nouveau jewelry. The piece must sparkle with quality if it is presented as an excellent piece of the period and particularly if it is quite expensive. The design and composition must be appealing and must contribute to the overall appearance of a quality piece. Size is an important factor, but even small pieces can represent the best features of Art Nouveau, as is evidenced in many of the illustrations in this book. Each piece must be as critically evaluated as a painting. Does it move you, or does is seem merely a pleasing ornament? Do the colors blend or do they clash? Does the design appear to be static or in motion? Does the piece represent the philosophy of Art Nouveau in boldness, freedom, and imagination. The answers to these questions help determine whether or not the item is authentic Art Nouveau, and, if it is, just how much it may be worth.

Judging quality often depends on an individual's taste. To become skillful in judging quality, one should study good pieces of jewelry in museums, auction houses, private collections, etc. There can be no substitute for personal experience acquired through observation, study, and touch.

Design and Composition

Design and composition are probably the most important concrete factors that signify quality in Art Nouveau jewelry. The best designed pieces vividly portray the basic philosophy and the best techniques of Art Nouveau. Excellency in design determines the ultimate appeal of the subject of hte piece and the manner in which it is conveyed. The design must be appealing and it must incorporate and enhance the natural beauty of all of the materials used, especially in their relationship to one another. There must be a pleasant transition in color and substance that does not conflict. Innovative ideas must meet with the basic philosophy. Boldness, daring, and new ideas must be consistent with the tenets of Art Nouveau; they must show discipline and restraint. Figure 50, a rooster made by Lalique, is a good example of an important Art Nouveau design. The caption accompanying this photography explains why this piece of jewelry is extraordinary in quality and, as such, representative of the basic concepts of Art Nouveau in its design and workmanship.

Materials & Workmanship

Many new materials for making jewelry were introduced and others newly emphasized during the Art Nouveau period. Horn was mixed with gold and silver in exquisite hair combs and dragonflies. *Pâte de verre* and glass were molded into captivating shapes and colors and combined with precious metals and gems. Ivory was sculptured and baroque pearls blended into the curves and colors of the overall design. Uncut gemstones and pale-colored semi-precious stones were used to provide subtle beauty and mystique. Even miniature impressionistic paintings on ivory were incorporated into Art Nouveau settings. Practically all these materials can be found in expensive and very inexpensive Art Nouveau jewelry pieces. In all but the cheapest commercial pieces, the workmanship was reasonably good and the piece provided a sense of beauty and "of the period" charm not evident in new reproductions.

In an item that is made of gold, both the quality and the workmanship are important factors in determining its worth. First, check the purity of the gold. If a dealer says that a certain piece is French Art Nouveau and it is stamped "14 carat," something is wrong. French Art Nouveau jewelry must be at least 18 carat gold and it must have an eagle's head stamp on it to confirm this. Occasionally the clasp of a pin may have been removed and subsequently replaced with a 14 carat one, but the major portion of a piece of French Art Nouveau jewelry must be 18 carat gold. If a piece is declared American Art Nouveau, it may be stamped 10 carat, 14 carat, or 18 carat (especially if it was made by Tiffany, Marcus & Company, or Kohn).

Practically all good French Art Nouveau pieces have a familiar type of gold work with sculpturing effects both on the front and back. The surface of the gold usually appears to be soft and wavy and is rarely brightly polished. There should not be large numbers of obvious pits in the metal that arise from improper casting. Of utmost importance is the finishing detail of all good pieces; it should be virtually the same on both front and back. The edges of the gold work should be generally rounded and not sharp. Usually the gold work is not as precise and perfect as that found in the work of Fabergé. Most gold work in French Art Nouveau is more graceful, free flowing, and pleasant than that found in Fabergé's work. Reproductions and revival pieces fail to show the excellent quality so characteristic of the goldsmithing of the French Art Nouveau jewelers.

Fine pieces of French jewelry are being reproduced and styles revived. Recently made reproductions of American Art Nouveau jewelry are also appearing in the marketplace. Careful examination of the enameling will uncover a marked difference between authentic Art Nouveau jewelry and these newly produced pieces. The Art Nouveau jewelers had a remarkable ability to shade enamel and to blend one shade into another that is extremely difficult to emulate in modern workshops. By studying the older pieces it is possible to determine the shortcomings of copies and revival items, whose enameling is more precise and uniform, less artistic and new looking. No substantial efforts have been made to reproduce British jewelry in the Arts and Crafts style and this is probably because pieces in this style have not risen sufficiently in price to justify such efforts.

Much Art Nouveau jewelry is fragile and easily damaged. It is often enameled and this enameling is frequently in the delicate *plique à jour* style. Many pieces were made to be looked at and loved, and not necessarily to be worn or handled like ordinary jewelry. Many of these items were broken and are in poor condition because a coat or sweater may have been worn over them. Such damage reduces their value and, of course, detracts from their beauty. A large defect is unacceptable; a small one generally can be overlooked. It is difficult to repair broken enamel and poor repairs are also unacceptable; a repair should be done well or not at all. One should not hesitate in accepting a broken piece that has been skillfully repaired. Frequently a piece of jewelry shows ungainly repairs with cold solder which detracts seriously from its appearance and value.

All jewelry should be studied carefully to determine if it is in excellent condition or if it has been repaired. Sometimes there is evidence that an entire section has been added from another piece of jewelry in order to fill in a break. This is a serious flaw since the piece is now merely an amalgamation or "put together."

Many times a piece of jewelry has been converted from a brooch to a pendant or a necklace. Such a conversion requires the removal of the pin and the subsequent addition of two gold loops. This procedure does not detract significantly from the beauty or the value of the piece. However, occasionally the removed pin or clasp contained the maker's mark and its removal destroyed the identification mark of the artist. Collectors almost unanimously discourage such alterations of beautiful pieces. There are many ways of adapting jewelry for wear without destroying its original condition.

Marks

In general, the marks on Art Nouveau jewelry help to establish the authenticity of the pieces. These tiny marks on jewelry can tell much about the piece: the purity of the gold or silver used in its composition; its country of origin or import; the name of the designer; when the piece was made; and so on. There are now on the marketplace newly made pieces of Art Nouveau Jewelry stamped with the name of Lalique and Fouquet. These names have also been recently stamped or engraved on old pieces of Art Nouveau jewelry that were made by others and not marked. The buyer must learn to distinguish these irregularities and not be misled. Lalique's stamp, for example, has many characteristic features which are not evident in the faked "signatures." The subject of marks is treated at length in a separate section of this book.

Enameling

The enameling in fine pieces of Art Nouveau jewelry reflects the skill and efforts of master enamelers. Fine enameling requires careful planning and many hours of hand work. It is usually shaded in a subtle and delightful manner; bubbles appear infrequently, but when they do they do not detract from the purity of the enamel nor the quality of workmanship. The enameling used in the newly produced pieces is much more uniform in appearance than that in authentic Art Nouveau pieces. Throughout this book are illustrations of the types of enameling used which will serve as a guide to authenticating the enameling work of outstanding masters.

Appearance on the reverse

Nearly all good handmade pieces exhibit the same fine finish on their reverse as is found on their front. The gold is engraved, chased, sculptured, and even enameled. It is not polished as though it just came off a press. The edges on the reverse side are polished and rounded but the surface is slightly irregular due to the hand pressure and instrumentation of the artist. On *plique à jour* and *cloisoné* pieces the gold and reticular work is also hand done.

Sculpturing

On gold pieces of jewelry particularly, the sculpturing of the figures is extremely important in authenticating works of the period. The sculpturing of the female heads with long flowing hair, the delicate flowers, and exotic birds and insects should be especially finely detailed and expressive. Many hours of tedious handwork were required to produce a finely sculptured piece of jewelry; a fine piece is generally not reproduced by a machine. Furthermore, the casting must be excellent and the enameling done in appealing colors, artistically shaded, and in good condition to highlight the features of the subject. Lastly, there must not be any conspicuous repairs.

Gemstones

For the most part, large and important gemstones were not used in Art Nouveau jewelry. The Art Nouveau jeweler emphasized artistry, setting, and enameling. Gems were used merely to highlight the design and to improve the overall composition. The color of the stones used was of particular importance. Opals, moonstone, small diamonds, semi-precious colored stones, and pearls were commonly used in Art Nouveau pieces. Very often insects, such as moths, butterflies, and dragonflies, were first enameled and then small stones were added to enhance their appearance. Fouquet's orchard (Figure 6), in which he used small diamonds to simulate dew drops, is an excellent example of the use of gemstones. He also made astonishing use of pink and silver baroque pearls in his lake and hills scene (Figure 7).

Summary

The following guidelines will be most helpful in determining if a piece of Art Nouveau jewelry is "of the period" or if it has been recently made.

On new pieces, the enameling will generally be uniform with sharp, precise edges, and it will have little or no shading. The piece itself will have a "new" appearance, with edges that are not rounded or worn. The pin and clasp will be in "mint" condition, showing little or no signs of wear. Rings, too, will have no indication of having been worn. File and polishing marks, indicative of handwork, will be missing. Hallmarks on gold pieces will also appear new and the settings for gems will be identical because they have generally been stamped out by machine. The reverse side of the jewelry will be smooth. Numerous pits in the gold will indicate careless casting. The sculpturing will not be artistic; the features will be poor and lack detail. Female figures will not be graceful and expressive. Finally, many similar pieces will be seen in the shops.

VII
Silver Art Nouveau Jewelry

Gold was the favorite material of the mid or High Victorian period. The symbol of prosperity, it was colored, wrought, chased, granulated, bloomed, and generally transformed by the mid-nineteenth century craftsman. Silver became more plentiful in the 1860s with the discovery of large deposits in the United States. Silver jewelry made before that time is comparatively rare; the metal was mainly reserved for the setting of diamonds. By the 1880s, new fashions, the introduction of electric lights, and the onset of the aesthetic movement combined to make colorless jewels and gems high fashion, and from the late 1880s and 1890s, silver was widely used for the new kind of mass-produced, inexpensive popular jewels in England, Germany, and especially the United States.

In England Art Nouveau had become synonymous with the Liberty & Co. style, and Liberty jewelry tells virtually the full story of English Art Nouveau jewelry. It was the first time silver jewelery took on an exclusively and individual, artistic appeal. The Arts and Crafts movement had worked almost totally in silver, gold being more expensive and also a more sumptuous, showy symbol of personal wealth and therefore rejected. It was essential to concentrate on inexpensive materials: the dulled, less glamorous appearance of silver was more in line with Arts and Crafts ethics and so was inherited by Liberty and its modern jewels.

Liberty's aim was, simply put, to bring jewels of fresh artistic merit to the general public, and, in accordance with Arts and Crafts doctrine, to disseminate artistic productions showing "individuality of idea and execution... a complete break with convention." Unlike Arts and Crafts devotees, however, Liberty was prepared to use the machine to achieve these ends, to create a wider appeal. Costs also had to be kept low for the success of the venture (although gold was still used fairly extensively by Liberty & Co.). In 1899, Liberty marketed their first items of Cymric silverware. Cymric was the registered trade name for their "modern" line of artistic jewels.

As the name suggests, Cymric was based on a Celtic revival style. Important elements combined to make the distinctive Liberty Art Nouveau style: interlacing and complex knot motifs, clear whiplash outlines, simple linear shapes, stylized leaves—all very strong lines with a controlled movement, more disciplined than the Art Nouveau "noodle."

To this style, Liberty added a new kind of enamel, usually pools of peacock-mingled blue and green, called *floating enamels.* The jewels could be set with turquoise or mother-of-pearl, but the cheaper silver brooches mostly relied on their enamel and their general form for decorative appeal. The idea was to keep prices within reach of most customers, but to give them artistic flair for their money. The formula hit the right market and was a great success. Small Cymric brooches were reasonably priced by the standards of the day, and each one was given a hand-hammered appearance and a hand finish for that proof of the individual artist's attention.

Very often, the same designs were repeated economically on buttons, hat pins, and cloak clasps. Buckles were very popular in silver and showed great variation in design. Liberty & Co. subcontracted to other firms who specialized in the mass production of silver jewels. Most of the Cymric jewelry was made by W.H. Haseler and Son, of Birmingham. In 1901, Haseler and Liberty formed a joint company, but often Liberty style silver jewels bear the mark of W.H. Haseler alone.

Murrle, Bennett & Co. was prolific in producing very good silver jewelry, in terms of original design and quality (see chapter IX). In contemporary advertisements, Murrle, Bennett claimed that their jewels were by "Artists of the Modern School." They incorporated many of the same Celtic elements of design and added their own hallmark, which was the use of pinhead rivets, also on hammered surfaces. It is possible that Murrle, Bennett manufactured some of Liberty's jewels and certainly used workshops in Pforzheim, Germany.

Connell was another English firm that tried to copy or compete with the Liberty style and success story. Connell advertised a range of silver jewels in the same "modern" style, as did so many unidentified jewelers and silversmiths.

Spreading the Art Nouveau net to cover wider audiences and markets, Charles Horner went one step further in the story of cheap, mass-produced English Art Nouveau jewelry. The firm is often labeled as a pioneer of totally commercial mass production methods. Mostly the jewels are made of silver and enamel, and bear the maker's mark *C.H.* The greater part were made later than the Liberty venture, most of them dating from the early years of the twentieth century. What made Horner a pioneer in his field was the fact that for the first time every stage of manufacture was carried out in his factory in Halifax in the North of England. Horner introduced more sophisticated machinery from Germany to become totally self-sufficient, and each piece, from design to finished product, was seen through in the factory.

It is interesting to note, with Horner's as with other forms of cheap silver Art Nouveau jewelry, how the original, often idealistic design elements were adapted to cater to mass consumption. Usually, designs were diluted into more acceptable form, less individualistic, less shockingly modern. Horner took the basic and most distinctive features of the Celtic design and then simplified them, softened them, and came up with a modern look that was not too avant-garde, easier to appreciate by a customer who did not want to identify with a complex art or social movement. The same can be said for adaptations of French Art Nouveau design in Germany and the United States.

Horner's standard designs consist of silver pendants, brooches, and hat pins—a specialty—characterized by mingled blue and green, (usually less intense than Liberty's version), blue and purple, green and yellow, or red and yellow enamels. The firm made simple knot brooches and plain silver jewelry, and introduced a rather stiff but attractive little winged scarab motif.

Swirls of enamel in colors that were bled into each other—blue, green, lime, yellow, and red—can be found in many variations on unmarked or unidentified inexpensive silver turn-of-the-century jewels. There were many freelance designers working at the time, another inheritance from the Arts and Crafts movement, and some of these were known for setting fashions while others followed and copied. Even traditional silversmiths like William Comyns made fashionable silver belt buckles in swirling floral Art Nouveau designs.

A good quantity of silver Art Nouveau jewelry was made in Germany around the turn of the century, often marked with a German silver quality mark such as 850.

Theodor Fahrner, generally recognized as one of the most prolific and enterprising Pforzheim manufacturers, produced very inexpensive silver Jugendstil jewelry as well as his more artistic lines. These contained the basic components of French Art Nouveau: wandering, sensuous lines (but more controlled), a young girl's head or profile with ample free-flowing hair, flowers, and leaves. Usually the female head was more stereotyped than in French examples, presenting a more acceptable face of sweet femininity. Silver was usually embellished with mother-of-pearl, subtly colored pools of enamel, or cabochon semi-precious stones. Basically, the French master's shocking interpretations of the female, the dying flower, or the nightmarish insect were forced into simple, less detailed versions by demands of public taste and of mass production.

Talking about Austrian jewelry at the turn of the century, W. Fred notes that "in modern decorative work, silver is now very largely used and appreciated." Elsa Unger is then praised for her skillful use of the material. She was the daughter of a well-known etcher, Professor William Unger. Elsa Unger is noted for her silver jewelry: she had a good feeling for the material and for how best to use it. She hammered, chiselled, engraved the metal, and added *plique à jour* enamels of "soft, harmonious colouring." She worked out her own designs and saw them through, which was obviously unusual at that time. W. Fred says that some of the pieces of jewelry such as gentlemen's studs or cuff links are in beaten silver with blue enamel, hair combs are of beaten silver and pale lilac enamel, showing a graceful blend of line and color. He describes them as "simple and elegant" and adds that they have "the rare advantage of being also cheap."

Several other Austrian designers chose to work in silver. Students at art schools learnt their craft practising on silver and achieved very successful artistic results. At that time, as with Liberty, it was possible to have a "real work of art, of which but few examples are produced at a very low price—say from about 35 shillings." These jewels were not mass produced.

In the United States, two main centers for mass production of commercial jewels in the nineteenth century were in Newark, New Jersey and Providence, Rhode Island. In both cases, the industry had started at the beginning of the nineteenth century and had grown enormously by the 1880s, and so was poised ready to spread the popularity of Art Nouveau jewels.

William B. Kerr & Co. was established in 1855 in Newark, New Jersey and produced silver tableware and gold personal accessories, as well as gold and silver jewelry. Demand for fashionable jewelry had increased considerably by this time, with the growth of the prosperous and always fashion-conscious middle classes. This silver jewelry was mostly made by a stamping process which looked like *repoussé* work, as if it had been hand-hammered or beaten into shape from the back. A limited range of motifs was used, but in many different combinations, to produce a large repertoire of jewels, all similar but different. The hollow shell would be backed with a thin sheet of silver to give an impression and appearance of weight and substance. According to Charlotte Gere, designs were copied from European periodicals which were widely used in the United States. Kerr produced these jewels in vast quantities, in a standardized French Art Nouveau style. This suited the huge demand for the latest fashions in European jewelry. In 1906, the firm was bought by the Gorham Company and moved to Rhode Island.

The Gorham Corporation was another American company that started the trend for home-produced jewelry instead of relying on European imports. Gorham began in the early nineteenth century in Providence, Rhode Island and was built up to a prosperous business particularly in the later years of the century when mass production was the perfect answer to an ever-growing demand from fashion-conscious sectors of society. In its early years, the firm was well known for "Gorham chain", which was of fine quality. In 1842, the founder Jabez Gorham took his son as a partner, renaming the firm Gorham Manufacturing Company. Jabez Gorham retired in 1847.

In a similar way to Charles Horner in England, Gorham was a pioneer in using mass production for silverware and at the turn of the century was ready to capture the new large jewelry markets. At this time a group of the most skilled silversmiths in the States was gathered together by Holbrook to work for Gorham. They were to make up the designs of another group of artists led by William C. Codman, an Englishman who had left his job with a silversmith in London to come to Providence in 1891. This is the most characteristic Gorham jewelry, with its hand-hammered finish, marketed under the appropriate trade name, "Martelé." Much inspiration came from French Art Nouveau designs, and also from the American branch of the Arts and Crafts movement. A range of Gorham jewelry was made in mixed metals, silver, silver gilt, and copper, set with fresh-water pearls or agates, or often with no stones at all, much after the manner of the aesthetic movement. It was a successful production line.

Very much of the same tradition of attractive mass-produced American Art Nouveau jewels is the firm of Unger Brothers, also of Newark, New Jersey. Three brothers, Herman, Eugene, and Frederick, founded the firm in 1878 as H. Unger & Co. When Frederick died, the business became Unger Brothers, moving gradually to larger premises and keeping a New York Office at 192 Broadway. The family business became involved in Art Nouveau design when Eugene and his family visited the influential Exposition Universelle in 1901. Designs were patented some two years later by Philomen Dickinson, Eugene's chief designer and brother-in-law. These French-inspired designs were used, in a similar method to that of Kerr & Co., on brooches, buckles, and clasps, imitating *repoussé* work in flower and leaf designs, introducing the statuesque young girl's head or profile and flowing hair. It was inexpensive fashionable jewelry, usually in plain silver, some gilt, and set with semi-precious stones. Eugene died in 1909, and production of Art Nouveau silver ended in 1910.

Danecroft, Schiebler, and other firms also produced large numbers of silver jewelry in the Art Nouveau style.

The range of silver Art Nouveau jewelry is wide, from avant-garde German and modernistic Austrian designs, to English Liberty style and American stylized mass production of French ideas. All have their value in jewelry history, whether for design, production techniques, or a reflection of contemporary fashions.

VIII

English Arts and Crafts Jewelry

Arts and Crafts originated in England, emerging as a strong reaction against the worsening effects of mechanization felt quite early in the nineteenth century. The lament over industrialization in academic circles grew louder and was taken up by those pricked by a painful social conscience. They searched for ideals and models in medievalism and Renaissance art and life.

The writings of John Ruskin formed the basis of the movement and were read by William Morris and widely circulated by F.D. Maurice in his Working Men's College, started in 1854. The cause was strenghtened by the demoralizing display of machine-made, showy, and, in some views, tasteless goods at the Great Exhibition of 1851. It seemed then that it was impossible to produce a work of art under the present system.

From this undercurrent of academic revolt evolved a set of principles for a renewal of the crafts. Morris and his associates determined to bring more personal fulfillment and freedom of expression to the individual artist-craftsman, and through this to bring an enjoyment of true art to those people so oppressed by the machine. They believed the decline in artistic design stemmed from a social sickness, and they saw that their way to an idealistic social and moral reform lay through this therapeutic revival of the arts and crafts.

The areas of metalwork and jewelry were perhaps the most appropriate to the whole Arts and Crafts movement, and certainly had the most chance of achieving its ideals. The application of their principles to jewelry meant that all jewels were to be handmade. The craftsman had to be given the central role: in his workshop he designed, made, and decorated the jewel himself from start to finish. In reality this was not so practical. The amateur could rarely attain the all-around skills required, nor match the perfection of technique of the specialist worker; neither could he come up to the expectations of rivalling the standards of Leonardo de Vinci or Botticelli, who was believed to have been an equally talented goldsmith. It simply was not possible to revive the Renaissance man in a different age. Also, the handmade object was more expensive than the machine-made equivalent, and in any case, people did not really want jewels that to them looked amateurish, dull, and old-fashioned. Defeating the whole object, the pieces appealed to a small elite group educated into this aesthetic approach. Ironically, the designs that were most successful in reaching the people were those adapted for the machine, produced cheaply and in large quantities, and professionally finished. This was most successfully accomplished by Liberty & Co. It was the total rejection of the machine that limited the hoped-for spread of art and ideals.

The formation of English guilds and art schools during the 1880s was an important part of the social and artistic movement. Guilds were set up on co-operative principles to create handmade goods, to provide workshops where amateurs could learn and experiment. The first co-operative was the Guild of St. George, set up by Ruskin in 1871; it was a trial of a democratic system, not really suited to such a strong personality as John Ruskin's, but it paved the way for other guilds that were central to the continuation of the movement. Next, the Century Guild was established by architect and designer A. H. Mackmurdo in 1882; the Art Workers Guild in 1884; and, as an extension, the Arts and Crafts Exhibition Society was formed in 1888 and exhibitions held in 1888, 1889, and 1890. The most important guild for jewel design was the Guild of Handicrafts, founded by C. R. Ashbee in 1888, with three members and a capital of 50£.

Birmingham was also an important centre of Arts and Crafts jewelry. The Birmingham Guild of Handicraft was founded in 1890, involving many of the leading metalworkers. The Artificers Guild was founded in 1901 by Nelson Dawson, and this also specialized in metalwork and jewelry. From this it is clear that jewelry played an important part in the general output of the movement.

Leading figures

Many of the leading artists, including the names mentioned here, worked as teachers in the large number of art schools that started at the height of the movement. It is very important for collectors to consider that there were numerous students working very closely in the manner of their teachers—a characteristic of the movement—and much of the jewelry found today could well be student work.

Jewelers in the Art and Crafts movement rarely signed their work, and this also makes attributions difficult and vague, but gradually styles of particular makers came to be recognized.

Charles Robert Ashbee (1863–1942), a self-taught silversmith and jeweler, is perhaps the best known. Having established his Guild and School of Handicraft in the East End of London, he later moved the Guild workshops to Chipping Camden, Gloucestershire, keeping retail outlets in London. Working in a country village was more in line with Arts and Crafts ideals; manufacturing in the city smacked of capitalism. Ashbee made good use of turquoise enamels, a kind of peacock blue, on his jewels and was keen on organic leaf shapes and the peacock motif. Edgar Simpson often followed Ashbee's style, and Fred Partridge, a skilled designer and jeweler, worked with Ashbee in Chipping Camden. His work particularly in horn, shows an unusual influence by French Art Nouveau. Ashbee is considered especially important in the story of Arts and Crafts and contributed to the development of Art Nouveau jewelry design and to later modern movements in Europe. Also, his influence can be seen in the work of several other Arts and Crafts workmen. Ashbee used the peacock motif to good effect, setting the feathers with mother-of-pearl, opals, or moonstones, and he is noted for a softly billowing four-petalled design. His use of this kind of sensual, organic plant interpretation and of moths and insects heralded the onset of Art Nouveau themes.

It is interesting that so many leading metalworkers trained originally as architects, such as Henry Wilson (1864–1934), chief assistant to J.D. Sedding, who turned to metalwork around 1890. He also wrote an important technical book called *Silverwork and Jewellery*. J. Paul Cooper (1869–1933) studied jewelry in Wilson's workshop and developed a similar style. He was one of the most successful Arts and Crafts jewelers, and was able to design and carry out his ideas with great skill and sensitivity. Arthur Gaskin (1862–1928) was an accomplished jeweler and worked with his wife Georgie creating a very distinctive style, using coils of gold or silver wire, flowers and leaves, and small colored stones. Alexander Fisher (1864–1936) was the foremost Arts and Crafts enamelist and an influential teacher of the subject. He was noted for his use of foil flecks or *paillons*. Enameling, particularly of flowers and birds, was also a specialty of Nelson Dawson (1859–1942) and his wife Edith, and they founded the Artificers Guild in 1901, where one of their fellow members was metalworker and designer Edward Spencer. Bernard Cuzner (1877–1956) was extremely talented and influenced by Gaskin, as one of the Birmingham group. Sometime about 1900 he was designing for Liberty & Co., along with other Arts and Crafts designers.

An expert enamelist and a fellower of Alexander Fisher, Phoebe Traquair achieved some remarkable results and is known for her enamels of a religious or spiritual nature. Enamel plaques by Traquair often decorated silver or copper boxes or caskets.

Some Liberty jewels can be included in this category, even though they were mass produced and commercial, as the firm did recognize and employ some of the best designers working within the Arts and Crafts framework, notably Archibald Knox (1864–1933), who made a major contribution to the movement and to the future of design. Knox began to work for Liberty sometime between 1895 and 1898, and then designed for their "Cymric" range. He was largely responsible for their Celtic revival, and he originated the widely imitated interlacing and whiplash motifs. Liberty also bought designs by Cuzner, Gaskin, and Oliver Baker. Oliver Baker is best known for superb buckles of distinctive design.

Materials and Forms of Jewelry

Ruskin's basic theories stipulated that materials should not be tampered with, and should be used as nearly as possible in their natural state. Materials were never chosen for their intrinsic value, but for colors, finish, and texture, and there was a conscious effort to create beauty from the least glamorous materials. J. P. Cooper, for example, used 15 carat gold simply because he liked its color. Stones were never or rarely faceted but were used as cabochons, and diamonds were completely shunned. Turquoises were particularly favored, especially when they were veined with brown matrix; the satin finish of mother-of-pearl was popular, and little baroque or river pearls often used as drops on pendants. Other simi-precious stones included moonstones, peridots, amethysts, opals, and the clear orange fire opals. Claw settings were rare, and the plain collet setting was preferred. Silver was far more widely used than gold, and was often hand beaten or hammered or chased into tiny leaves, flowers, or coils of wire. Arts and Crafts jewels were always handmade, with joints secured by wound wire, or flaps of metal tucked through slits and folded over at the back, often rather crudely. Pendants and necklaces were the most popular items, often seen with loops and festoons of chain. Many waist buckles and cloak clasps were also made, as they suited the concept of introducing art to a more functional object.

The revival of enameling, a Renaissance jewel feature, was a major feature of Arts and Crafts jewelry. The handmade product was in this case often better and more artistic than commercially produced enamels, so that enamel work was one of the more successful ventures of the movement. Charles Fleetwood Varley painted beautiful landscape enamels, usually mounted by Liberty as box lids and occasionally as jewels. He was one of a family of Victorian painters and created land and seascapes of murky and misty atmospheric scenes of deep colors and hazy light.

Enthusiasm for Arts and Crafts jewels can often lead to false ideas that the most characteristic and therefore the most obviously amateur and handmade are the best examples. When choosing, it is important to keep the same standards of judgement applied to other jewelry, looking carefully to see if the piece is well made, if the enameling is beautifully done, if the finish is good, and in all, trying to choose a piece of jewelry that bears a good balance between design, materials, and technique.

IX
German Art Nouveau Jewelry

Contrary to popular belief, not all French style Art Nouveau jewelry was produced in France. A great deal of good quality jewelry in strong Art Nouveau style was manufactured in Germany, principally in Pforzheim, a town on the edge of the Black Forest that centered then, as now, around the jewelry industry. Like Birmingham in England, Pforzheim became known for mass-produced commercial jewels, but there is much more to the story of Pforzheim jewel production than the churning out of stereotype designs.

The history of the town's unique jewelry museum, or "Schmuckmuseum", tells of the close association with Paris design at the turn of the century. The Arts Club and Art School of Pforzheim, founded in 1877, started to collect ancient jewels in the last quarter of the nineteenth century. Ancient goldwork and artifacts had captured the interest and fascination of European goldsmiths and the archaeological revival style that grew from this fascination became perhaps the most important aspect of Victorian jewel design. Everyone sought to own authentic ancient examples, some of which were brought back to Pforzheim to serve as models and inspiration for the town's numerous workshops. The ancient jewels acquired by the Arts Club also formed the basis of the Schmuckmuseum's present collection and started something of a tradition. Continuing the work of the Arts Club, Art Nouveau jewels were bought from Paris for the same purpose, to serve as models, and were incorporated into the new season's collections.

The grasping tentacles of Art Nouveau had reached Germany, which had its own version of the style called *Jugendstil*, a pure, if less imaginative, variation of French Art Nouveau. The name Jugendstil came from the magazine *Jugend*, or *Youth*, which was published in Munich. The Pforzheim industry with its professional skills and outlook turned an idealistic principle and major art movement into a successful chapter in the history of jewel design. It seems now that many so-called French Art Nouveau jewels may in fact have been made in Pforzheim. Relatively little is understood of the town's links with Paris, but some examples prove that there was an interchange of ideas and designs between the two. We know also that a strong link existed between Pforzheim and English Art Nouveau jewelry via the firm of Murrle, Bennett & Co. Another interesting and artistically important connection grew up with the town of Darmstadt and its artists' colony some 100 miles away.

Pforzheim is best known for its large numbers of mass-produced inexpensive and fashionable Jugendstil jewels. They were often made in low grade silver, with the familiar motif of the female head with flowing tresses of hair. Other firms meanwhile were producing gold jewels in the Art Nouveau style, which included beautifully chased brooches, pendants, and hat pins of ribboned gold, decorated with delicate pastel enamels in leaf, flower, or thistle motifs; pearls nestled in leaves or petals of opalescent-shaded enamels or *plique à jour*. Textured and colored goldwork showed Japanese inspiration, as did the carved horn of organic forms. They were all made in Pforzheim, perhaps for the French market. Certainly, the exchange of designs and ideas was as fluid as the Art Nouveau line.

Pforzheim manufacturers travelled to Paris to bring back ideas and designs, as well as actual models to copy, and it seems that some Parisian jewelers had jewels made, to specific designs, in Pforzheim. It is known that enamels by the French enamelist Tourette, who worked for Lalique, Vever, and Fouquet, were bought in Paris by a Pforzheimer who then organized a competition among Pforzheim workshops for a suitable frame. The Schmuckmuseum displays a brooch containing a Tourette enamel with a gold frame made by a second-prize winner Ruhle.

One of the best known jewelers is Theodor

Fahrner, certainly among the most important and most enterprising manufacturers in Pforzheim at the turn of the century. He was very successful in producing inexpensive but fashionable jewels. While other firms may have been in Paris chasing fashionable French Art Nouveau designs, Fahrner saw inspiration for a range of new "artistic" jewels nearer home. Germany had its own artists striving to promote a fresh, pure approach to art, and an artists' colony had been established under the patronage of the Grand Duke of Hesse at Darmstadt, not too far away from Pforzheim, to encourage those ideals and to bring talent together in an atmosphere removed from the suffocating pollution of industrialism. Some of the finest artists and architects of Germany and Austria had gathered there. The Grand Duke Ernst-Ludwig of Hesse was an art lover and particularly interested in seeing the growth of modern movements and in encouraging the development of young artistic talent. Josef Maria Olbrich, a leading figure in the Vienna Secession, was the Viennese architect commissioned to design and set up a colony which gathered a wealth of gifted artists and designers. The colony was built on the site of the Matildenhöhe, a hill in Darmstadt, and was dominated by the modernistic Marriage Tower, designed by Olbrich and built in 1901, an early prediction of Art Deco and enough to highlight the avant-garde influence that Darmstadt designers could bring to Pforzheim and to jewelry.

When the Darmstadt artists did turn to jewel design, it was Fahrner who executed most of them. He commissioned jewel designs from Patriz Huber, Olbrich, Moritz Gradl, Van de Veldé and Hubich, as well as leading Pforzheim designers such as Kleemann. Huber was important enough to have his initials marked alongside Fahrner's mark. His work was simple and is distinguished by the restrained, dull silver surfaces set with stones of subdued color or enamels. Moritz Gradl's designs made by Fahrner are unusual, distinctive, and sought after but rare; compared to those of Huber they show more variation, as well as increased color and movement. Fahrner developed his distinctive style to such an extent that it became known as *Fahrnerschmuck*, continuing well into the 1940s, and it is still well thought of in Pforzheim, although the firm is now no longer in existence.

While Fahrner was capitalizing on home-grown talent, another important and versatile firm, Zerrenner, excelled at French styles. The firm of Zerrenner is still in existence and thriving, having been established in 1843. Zerrenner was one of the leading manufacturers of Jugendstil jewelry. The owners often travelled to France to bring back ideas for the firm, and in those days they had their own designers to adapt ideas and also their own toolmakers.

Zerrenner produced Parisian style jewels in large quantities, which were often passed off as French work and sold in Paris as such. They looked just like the creations of Bing or Lalique. One basic difference, however, was that German forms and motifs were most often enclosed in a square, in contrast to the more open lines of the French. Keeping within the limits of their mechanical skills, Zerrenner copied French techniques of applied motifs to tortoise shell and Japanese-inspired goldwork. Zerrenner made a number of hat pins, brooches, and pendants which were naturalistic and colorful, using shaded translucent enamel in stylized, somewhat restrained forms. Another group of Zerrenner brooches in the Schmuckmuseum is inspired by Japanese mixed metalwork. One of the prize exhibits by Zerrenner is a pale tortoise shell hair comb with heavy-colored gold serpent and flower decoration. Completing a sketch of the versatile output of this firm are a few pieces that illustrate an elegant Edwardian style, including a brooch in silver gilt, entwined with ribbon and bow, laurel wreaths, and flowers set with tiny diamonds. Their success with such pieces emphasizes the ability of the German firms to turn their hand to any prevailing jewelry fashion and throws into question the certainty of national characteristics and attributions.

Another family firm of Pforzheim jewelers, the Gebrüder Falk (Falk Brothers), designed and made good quality gold and silver gilt jewels, beginning mainly with the kind of pendants that contained mirrors. They also made medallions, charms, and brooches and moved away from floral or sterotyped female motifs to explore the flowing shapes of dancers. They used the iris motif, a favorite of Lalique and one found frequently decorating Pforzheim jewels. Most of the designs were made by Fritz Falk; the administration was looked after by Heinrich Falk. Fritz Falk was a leading member of the Pforzheim Arts and Crafts Society, and a member of the family is now a director of the Schmuckmuseum. The firm was founded in 1897 and closed in 1926.

Louis Fiessler and Company is a firm that still exists today, founded in 1857 by Louis Fiessler. In

1892 the firm was sold by Fiessler's widow, and in 1919 the families Fuhrmann and Schaible took over and still own the firm. At the turn of the century Fiessler concentrated on high quality production and their jewels show the French connection quite clearly, with a highly individual use of plant forms. One gold pendant, molded as a girl's head framed by flowing locks of hair, can be compared to a pendant by the French master Lucien Falize.

Emil Riester (d. 1925/6) was a professor at the *Kunstgewerbeschule* (Arts and Crafts School) in Pforzheim, as well as an exciting jewel designer. His designs were often made up by Wilhelm Feucht, marked by the joined initials *WF.* He worked mainly in naturalistic forms, ranging from simple floral designs, a stunning large openwork butterfly brooch, to typically German linear pendants.

Georg Kleemann surely ranks as one of the leading Pforzheim jewelry designers of the early twentieth century. Born in 1863, Kleemann was a professor at the Arts and Crafts School from 1887 as a painter and jewelry designer. His designs were executed by craftsmen at the school, and in smaller numbers by leading names such as Lauer and Wiedmann, Fahrner, Zerrenner, C.W. Muller, Victor Mayer, and others. He is best known for his version of the flying beetle, the winged scarab motif. His creations were set with opals, emeralds, rubies, topaz, diamonds, with *plique à jour* enamel wings, and large bulbous mother-of-pearl or turquoise bodies.

Good German jewel design was not however totally exclusive to Pforzheim, and in other cities French style Art Nouveau jewels of very fine quality were emerging.

The best known jeweler in the French style is perhaps Robert Koch (1852–1902), who worked in Baden-Baden and in Frankfurt am Main. His work is recognized by the fine dog collar plaques, very much in the French manner, with winged sycamore seed motifs, in *plique à jour* enamel and a fine enameled lakeside view. Hermann Hirzel was designing slightly more Germanic, stylized jewels, produced in Germany by Louis Werner. Sculpted gold brooches using the female form were designed by Theodor von Gosen and executed by the Vereinigte Werkstätte in Munich. Lowenthal was a firm that executed important designs by Olbrich.

Austrian jewelry had been totally under the influence of Paris until the turn of the century when parallel modernistic art movements began to produce a new and distinctive style. In his treatise on modern Austrian jewelry published in a special edition of *Studio*, called "Modern Design in Jewelry and Fans," W. Fred says: "Now at last, however, the liberating influence of the modern spirit is making itself felt in the art of jewelry, as in everything else; and every ornament produced, whether in precious stones or in enamel, bears the unmistakable impress of the distinctive psychic character of our capital city, which even foreigners do not fail to recognise." He adds that the culture of Vienna is essentially feminine and recalling the essence of French Art Nouveau style says, "The graceful and witty, yet dreamy and passionate girls and women of Vienna give to it its distinctive character."

So long under the French influence, flowers were important in Austrian design, now achieving a balance between being artistic as well as true to nature. Roset and Fischmeister were experts in this realm.

Roset and Fischmeister were also noted and praised for their figural ornaments and sculptural work. Enamels and semi-precious stones were more widely used than precious stones, color and line being the most crucial elements, except perhaps in the work of Gustav Gurschner. Gurschner was basically a talented sculptor, and for him, form was the most important feature. W. Fred describes his nude figures as full of "childlike innocence and nervous strength," with the addition of a "spiritual expression."

Otto Prutsher is another important Austrian designer associated with a distinctive look not dissimilar in feel to Kleemann's work. He introduced more color in the form of enamels than most other designers. Josef Hoffman (1870–1956) was the founder of the Wiener Werkstätte in 1903, and an architect and designer who contributed enormously to twentieth century design. He has to be included in any study of Art Nouveau, but took a step away from the essence of Art Nouveau towards the modern style and its rejection of superfluous ornament. He designed a number of pieces of jewelry executed by the Wiener Werkstätte.

German Influence via Murrle, Bennett & Co.

The story of Liberty & Co. and Archibald Knox, their chief designer, is well documented and its importance to the progress of modern design well appreciated. Arthur Lazenby Liberty was a shrewd businessman with an exceptional talent for spotting new fashions in embryo, and for recognizing and capitalizing on creative designers. As a young man he anticipated the huge impact of Japanese arts and crafts and in 1875 he opened his own Oriental Emporium selling imported oriental wares.

Success led Liberty to trust his own business sense and he commissioned exclusive designs from various craftmen, for Liberty's famous fabrics and later silver and metalware. At this time the Arts and Crafts movement was struggling for recognition. Liberty saw the talent and potential in the leading Arts and Crafts designers. In the late 1890s he launched the Cymric metalworking venture which produced a range of mass-produced gold and silver jewels in unconventional and avant-garde designs. "Individuality of idea and execution" was the theme by which the new artistic and aesthetic approach was brought to the public in an acceptable and affordable package. Archibald Knox was responsible for the initial success of the Cymric venture, and for Liberty's Celtic revival.

The success of Cymric jewels led to rivalry and other versions of these so-called modern jewels and there are many unmarked and unidentified examples to prove this. The most distinctive and attractive parallel to Liberty jewelry is the work produced by a firm called Murrle, Bennett & Co. The similarities between Liberty and Murrle, Bennett designs led many people to believe that Murrle, Bennett & Co. plagiarised Liberty's designs. A large part of Murrle, Bennett's output seemed to consist of near copies of Liberty jewels. One silver pendant taken from a Knox design bears the Murrle, Bennett mark, suggesting a more concrete connection between the two firms.

Research has revealed that far from copying Liberty, Murrle, Bennett & Co. may well have instigated some of the most avant-garde and artistically imported designs, and this in turn has shed new light on the role of Pforzheim in interpreting designs for European markets.

The German link with Murrle, Bennett comes from the fact that Ernst Mürrle was a Pforzheimer. He came to work in London around 1880 for a compatriot in the jewelry trade. When Mürrle started his own business he kept close ties with Pforzheim, where he went at least six times a year on business and where he worked with his schoolfriends, Fahrner and Wilhelm Führer. There is a distinct parallel between the situation of Liberty and his involvement with Arts and Crafts designers and Fahrner's use of artists of the Darmstadt colony. Added to this, there was a close business tie between Farhner and Murrle, Bennett, and both their marks are often found together on the same piece of jewelry. There was an interchange of designs which meant that many Murrle, Bennett jewels may have derived from important designs by, for example, Patriz Huber or Gradl or possibly Olbrich. Murrle, Bennett also sold to France and had many interests in various countries throughout the world. All information points to the fact that Murrle, Bennett was more likely to have supplied Liberty with their jewels, which perhaps could be made more cheaply and more skillfully in Pforzheim workshops. There was certainly no need whatever for Murrle, Bennett to copy Liberty's designs.

There are several different styles of Murrle, Bennett jewels, some, as we have pointed out, looking exactly like Liberty models in silver with floating enamels and Celtic ornament. Others are far more German in character, in the Jugendstil manner, highly stylized and well designed. There is the dull aesthetic finish to the silver, controlled swirls and coils as settings to opaque green or red cabochon stones, triangular shapes or open conjoining circles, and organic-looking, irregularly shaped "cells" of translucent enamels. The most characteristic of the firm are the jewels of gold or silver, set with mother-of-pearl, amethyst, or turquoise. The gold has a rich creamy matt surface. Many are set with very large stones, especially turquoises which were often amply veined in black and brown. Large misshapen pearls were popular, and occasionally opal was used or striped black and onyx. Some of the gold work is Celtic inspired, with flowing outlines tapering into narrow gold wires, interlaced or trailing cage-like over the stone. Other features include the gold and silver "stitches" that sew two parts together, and the tiny pinhead bumps that look like rivet heads— both features most likely being derived from the fashion for hand-craftsmanship. Some gold jewels make good use of strong straight lines, probably influenced by German designs of the period seen at the first Secession Exhibition in Vienna of 1898.

There seems to have been an almost unique interchange and flow of designs and ideas in Europe, at a time when each country was developing, often for the first time, its own national identity in artistic jewelry design.

X
American Art Nouveau Jewelry

Tiffany was the foremost company producing works in the Art Nouveau style in the United States. In 1893 Tiffany took part in the Columbian Exposition exhibiting a Victorian type of jewelry that featured natural stones consistent with the style Tiffany had used for many years. These works showed the influences of Japanese art and French design modified for the American taste. Tiffany & Co. documented the merchandise produced for the Columbian exhibition in its annual catalogue known as the "Little Blue Book," which showed many types of jewelry, watches, flatware, and tableware. The first item of jewelry listed in this catalogue was an aquamarine and diamond three-piece tiara set, produced in a conventional style incorporating shells and seaweed. The piece featured 147 aquamarines and 1848 diamonds, with the enameled gold which was popular at this time in Europe. The tiara set was so unique it initiated a major difference in Tiffany jewelry. Also listed in the catalogue were many other items quite different from previous Tiffany work, including snake bracelets, enameled combs, and pieces of jewelry combining enamel with various stones. There were pieces in insect forms, including a caterpillar and a butterfly pin, as well as some using baroque pearls in the shapes of animals. This type of jewelry demonstrated a Japanese influence but some of the Tiffany designs incorporated artistry developed by the American Indians in their pottery, jewelry, and basketry.

In 1893 Tiffany was an old, established house of jewelry that used stones in a magnificent array of designs with various colored golds, but not with the natural appearance attainable by combining enamels with gold and colored gemstones.

Previous works had used only diamonds, emeralds, and rubies, but now they began using semiprecious stones that changed the color content of the works. This was a departure from the original Tiffany & Co. designs—newer and more exciting than anything they had produced before.

In 1902 Louis Tiffany came into the company as its artistic director after the death of his father. His influence began Tiffany's venture into Art Nouveau jewelry. Louis Tiffany had used explicitly Art Nouveau designs in his previous works of glass and bronzes. Prior to his liaison with Tiffany & Co. his works were signed "Tiffany Studios." Once he became a part of Tiffany & Co. his works bore the firm name. Tiffany & Co.'s pieces began to exhibit a flamboyant style similar to that of a punch bowl Louis Tiffany had exhibited at the Paris Exhibition in 1900. He now applied his distinctive style to the design of jewelry, using semi-precious and hard stones. His preference for American turquoise resulted in the purchase of a turquoise mine in the southwest in order to supply his increasing demand for the stone. He used demantoids with a great flourish. He combined opals with black stones and enamel, which was a unique new style. He enhanced lapis lazuli with sapphires. In all his endeavors he used every stone to its greatest advantage, enameling in colors to contrast and compliment each jewelry piece. Reminiscent of his previous work with glass scarabs embedded in bronze vases, lamp bases, and pottery, he now began mounting glass scarabs in 18 carat gold for both men's and women's jewelry. Perhaps the type of jewelry for which he is best known, however, is the making of cuff links, pendants, and other pieces from sections of colored glass mounted in 18 carat gold. Louis Tiffany's influence began to be reflected in silverware and tea services produced by other designers in the company. In this way, Louis Tiffany was responsible for inspiring Art Nouveau jewelry in New York to its highest level.

By 1904 Louis Tiffany began exhibiting on an international level. His first exhibition was in St. Louis in 1904. It contained more than twenty pieces of jewelry which he had either designed himself or rough designed in order that craft workers within the company could create pieces in his style. The pieces remaining from this exhibition in St. Louis were accumulated and sent to Paris for the 1905 Salon Exhibition. These and other pieces created specifically for that exhibition won international acclaim for Louis Tiffany. From this time on, all jewelry created in Louis Tiffany's artistic jewelry department was listed separately in the "Blue Book" under the heading of "Artistic Art Jewelry." This jewelry was all designed and produced under the personal supervision of Louis Tiffany, and each piece was unique. The most remarkable feature of these works were obtained in the combination of gold and enamel with precious and semi-precious stones. His work was known internationally and won great honors at various fairs.

Throughout Louis Tiffany's entire career he pursued an anti-classic style utilizing various cultural forms including Celtic, Islamic, and Japanese variations in the course of searching for new designs. His anti-classical style was a continuing theme in his bronzework, interior decoration, jewelry, and glass. This gave him a style distinct from anyone else creating in that period of American art history or in the entire Art Nouveau movement.

Tiffany art jewelry.

Tiffany's competitors were Stueben and a company known as Marcus Jewelry. Stueben's works can be differentiated from Louis Tiffany's in that they did not possess the color combinations and flamboyancy that Tiffany achieved in every design that he created. Marcus Jewelry used similar stones to those of Tiffany, in combination with enamel, gold, platinum, and diamonds. However, Marcus's Art Nouveau jewelry did not integrate the stones within the design or use the daring mountings that distinguish Louis Tiffany's designs. Tiffany's Art Nouveau jewelry is outstanding in that it absolutely sparkles and seems to reflect a life from within the piece. In contrast to Steuben glass, Tiffany glass was based on non-classical design and a richness in the form. Stueben glass was consistently of a classical design. In a similar way Marcus Jewelry reflected the past rather than anything decidedly new. Marcus did make some outstanding Art Nouveau pieces of platinum and enamel and developed

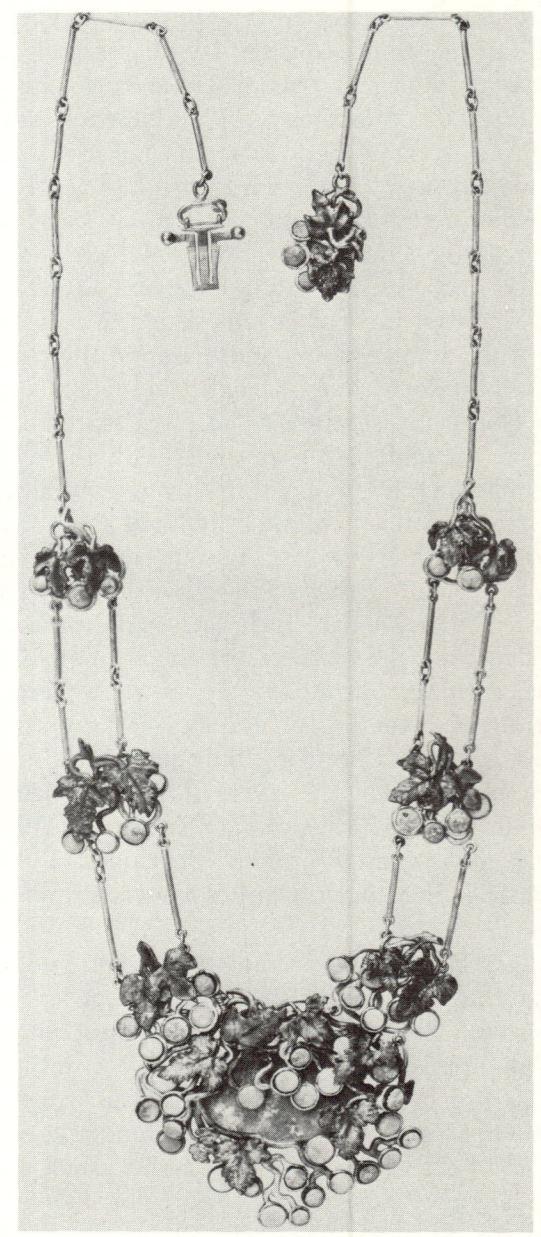

Necklace of gold, opals, and enamel in grape motif, designed by L. C. Tiffany for Tiffany & Co., ca. 1905.

a characteristic style of enameling using especially the colors of green and blue. He was a master of obtaining beauty from blemished or deformed stones and pearls.

Although Louis Tiffany continued to have his own Tiffany Studios after the onset of his position as director of art jewelry at Tiffany and Co., he sold all of his jewelry through Tiffany and Co. because it had catered to many multi-millionaires in its past history, as well as to the royalty of Europe, and Tiffany did not want to lose the kind of patronage.

One of Tiffany's workers who had helped to establish the jewelry department at Tiffany Studios was Julia Sherman. She had studied the Arts and Crafts workers in England and was an admirer of William Morris in England, and had also written about the Arts and Crafts movement there. She came to New York from New Jersey to work for Tiffany and helped him with his work at Tiffany Studios in ceremics, metals, and enamels. When he became the director of art jewelry at Tiffany and Co. he brought her with him. She was put in charge of the enameling and the jewelry setting within the artistic department, working primarily from Louis Tiffany's designs. However, she continued producing many works on her own as she had done at Tiffany Studios. They worked very well together and she stayed there until her marriage. Although Tiffany had other workers, Julia's pieces are distinctive and identifiable because they represent her workmanship, craftmanship, and taste incorporated in Louis Tiffany's designs. Unfortunately, Julia never put a jeweler's mark on a piece of jewelry that she created and it was all considered the work of Louis Tiffany.

There were other prestigious jewelers in the United States during the Art Nouveau period, including Alling and Co. of New Jersey. They did enamel pieces of Art Nouveau jewelry and some very fine sculptural pieces. Their work primarily consisted of miniature pieces such as men's stick pins and small pins for women's shirt collars. Their enameling was at a level with the French and of very fine quality.

Bailey, Banks & Biddle from Philadelphia worked mostly in traditional jewelry. However, they did use some very fine precious and semi-precious stones and were meticulous in their method of designing and in their settings. They produced very little Art Nouveau jewelry.

Battin & Co. of Newark, New Jersey produced small pieces of Art Nouveau jewelry that are still available on the market.

Ballou & Co. from Providence, Rhode Island produced small pieces of Art Nouveau jewelry, usually stamped out, but they were not outstanding works.

This large mushroom brooch was made by H. G. Murphy, an outstanding British goldsmith and enamelist who worked under Henry Wilson. The bright, contrasting enamel is set with a fire opal and diamonds. On the reverse is a brilliant green enamel characteristic of Murphy's work.

Birks & Co. in Canada, under the direction of artist Church Warden, Pike was an outstanding firm, but they did not emphasize any Art Nouveau design. Their pieces are hallmarked with a Lion and a *BB* on it.

Black, Starr & Frost also produced jewelry in a limited quantity of Art Nouveau but their work was not very outstanding.

Caldwell & Co. of Philadelphia was a very fine jewelry house using precious stones and semi-precious stones. They did some Art Nouveau pieces with enameling, but these are most rare.

Cummings & Co. from Attleboro, Massachusetts stamped out pieces of small jewelry in the Art Nouveau style. These were a simplification, using dyes to stamp out the designs (a common practice among goldsmiths who did not want to create any distinctive designs, but wanted to keep up with the style).

Durand & Co. of Newark, New Jersey produced small pieces of Art Nouveau in a similar fashion.

Gorham & Co. of Providence, Rhode Island was a major silver company who did some gold jewelry in the Art Nouveau style. Most of their Art Nouveau jewelry was in sterling silver and they used floral patterns and variations on a flower which were also stampings. Gorham eventually was one of the leading producers of Art Nouveau silver in large pieces. Those were Martelé designed pieces and of the finest quality of Art Nouveau silver produced in the United States.

Hedges & Co. was from New York and also made Art Nouveau jewelry. They are known for their small pieces with exceptionally fine enameling.

Krementz & Co. from Newark, New Jersey did an exquisite job of enameling in their jewelry during the Art Nouveau period. Their 14 carat gold jewelry was also very well finished. They were usually stamped out, but they were of a very fine quality and are still in existence.

Riker Brothers from Newark, New Jersey made a large quantity of Art Nouveau gold jewelry. The pieces were beautifully enameled and their technique was probably the most superb in this country. Unfortunately, they are signed with a mark resembling an *RL*, which led people to believe it was the work of René Lalique.

Heavy gold pendant with flesh and pastel colored enamels.

A major producer of Art Nouveau jewelry was William B. Kerr of Newark, New Jersey. This company came into existence in 1855. Their original trademark was a fleur de lis, but at some point they changed their trademark to a fasces. This label was either applied in sterling silver to the back of a piece or was impressed into the piece itself. William B. Kerr & Co. was known for its tableware and its sterling silver dresser sets. The designs were very French in style, with *repoussé* pieces of jewelry and equally deeply impressed pieces in their dresser sets. Early in the company's history it made gold dresser sets. Because they were very early in production they may have been of a classical Victorian style. The Art Nouveau pieces, to the best of the author's knowledge, are entirely in sterling silver. Kerr's Art Nouveau designs portrayed exquisite women with long flowing hair and smiling faces. The outstanding feature of his work was the depth of the features in each face and the realistic facial expressions. Pieces were stamped out and chased in such a fashion that every feature and each hair seemed to be clearly distinguished. This was in the style of the French Art Nouveau of 1900, and the women's faces were reminiscent of Mucha women. In addition to small pieces of jewelry, William B. Kerr & Co. made large dresser sets with the same females portrayed on them. They also produced dress belts which were a series of little plaques of the same face and the buckle formed of two opposing profiles. The plaques were connected by chains and may originally have contained silk ribbon holding them into solid form other than the chain. Kerr's workmanship was of superior quality and certainly reflected the highest principles of the Art Nouveau period.

In 1906 the Kerr Company was bought out by Gorham & Co. and moved to Rhode Island in 1907. The works combining the ideas of both Martelé and Kerr produced jewelry that was an outstanding example of the period.

As can be seen from the companies mentioned, Newark, New Jersey was one of the major centers of silversmithing at the turn of the century. It was in Newark that Tiffany silver was produced. Here, both Gorham and Kerr were located. In fact, virtually all of the silver companies were in this location except for a few in Massachusetts and Rhode Island. In this way silversmithing was confined to the New England area in the United States.

Unger Brothers was another company located in Newark. The company existed only between 1892 and 1909, but in this short-lived period they produced much great Art Nouveau jewelry. They began by producing small pieces for men, such as pocket knives and match safes. Their early production was rather limited, but in the year of the Paris Exhibition, Unger Brothers visited France and found sources for new designs. They incorporated the best of the French designs with their own silverware, making dresser sets in the form of a body, with arms upraised or picking or smelling flowers. In pins and brooches they used women's heads in simple plaques rounded by Art Nouveau floral borders to create an irregular outer edge. In addition, Unger Brothers made barrettes and hat pins, but these pieces were not as flamboyant as their dresser sets and other items where the space was greater. To improve their design yet keep within the French manner of Art Nouveau, they used borders on the edges to create irregular and freer forms. The only pattern that Unger Brothers used for a full set of flatware was the Douvaine, however they did a variety of smaller dessert forks and spoons using women's heads and bodies as the design. They took out patents for all their other Art Nouveau designs listing styles such as "Love's Dream," "Love's Voyage," "Stolen Kiss," "Indian," and "Chilly Cupids." They specialized more in an Art Nouveau "Indian" rather than just an American Indian. Unger Brothers tried including stones in some of their silver pieces, but these were not the most successful of their designs. Unger Brothers came into existence as an Art Nouveau entity at the turn of the century and unfortunately disappeared suddenly from the marketplace when the last owner had a horseback accident and was killed in 1909. At the time of his death, they had produced a catalogue which included innumerable items in the styles and patterns of Art Nouveau. Among them were dresser sets involving over twenty or twenty-five pieces and often including cut glass jars with silver covers. The catalogue also listed some rather daring smoking sets consisting of small ashtrays, match safes, cigarette boxes and cigarette cases portraying a woman with flowing hair holding a lit cigarette in her hand. Unger Brothers did produce some gold jewelry in Celtic design similar to that of Tiffany; however gold pieces are rather rare, as they worked predominantly in silver. Unger Brothers' pieces can be identified by a jeweler's mark consisting of a *UB*, one letter superimposed on the other.

At the turn of the century, Chicago had an Arts

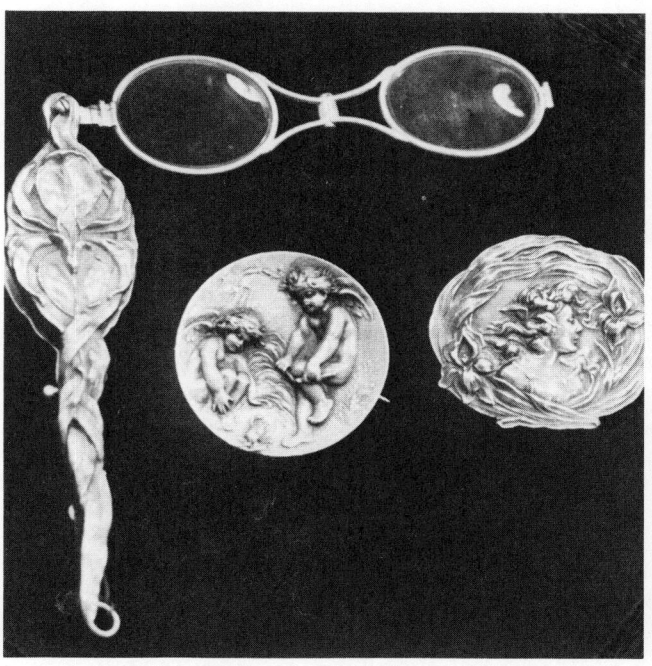

Lorgnette and two brooches in sterling silver, by Unger Brothers, ca. 1905.

and Crafts movement similar to that in England that formed a major part of the Art Nouveau movement there. There were many small centers in Chicago with craft workers and metalworkers involved in producing pieces unique in appearance. Marshall Field developed its own department of craft workers very much like Liberty & Co. in London, and their craftsmen produced designs that were sold bearing the company name. Of the many craft centers in Chicago, some produced a craft type of Art Nouveau jewelry. This type of jewelry is freer in form and of anti-classic design worked in semi-precious metals such as plated brass and copper, as well as pewter and silver. They used oxidation to turn brass black and their designs were well executed. They rarely worked in gold, as silver was quite plentiful and gold was expensive and commonly reserved for the work of formal jewelry companies.

Mrs. F. H. Koehler made jewelry and very fine Arts and Crafts pieces at the turn of the century. They were exhibited at various craft shows and sold at the Christmas holidays.

Foglioti made some very fine pieces of jewelry. His was among a number of studios that were connected with the Chicago Art Institute. Potter-Mellen and Lebolt in Chicago also produced Arts and Crafts style jewelry

Mathias William Hank was one of the larger companies making jewelry using stones in their natural forms, such as baroque pearls and sweetwater pearls, as well as various stones that were normally considered misshapen and not usable. This was common in the craftsman's jewelry in Chicago.

Kalo produced gold jewelry in a more sophisticated type of the Arts and Crafts design. They used semi-precious stones and baroque pearls, but they used them in combination with gold. Kalo pieces are rare because they were produced in only small quantities during the Chicago Arts and Crafts movement. Unique to this movement was the lack of sex discrimination. Women were employed on an equal level as both metalsmiths and designers in their various departments.

Many times the work of various craftsmen was sold through other jewelry companies in the Chicago area. Because the craftsmen hand made each item and had limited materials, they produced their works in very limited quantity. Thus, it was more profitable to sell through a larger company. One such company was Peacock & Co. It was founded by Elijah Peacock and managed by family members until as late as 1970. Elijah Peacock established himself as a watch repairman at the age of nineteen, sharing a small frame building with his brother Joseph, who, with a friend named David Thatcher, sold firearms. All three had emigrated from England where the Peacock family had been in the jewelry business for generations.

Peacock & Company, which became one of Chicago's major jewelry stores, produced little of its own merchandise, acquiring most of it from manufacturers and independent metalsmiths. It often double marked its goods with the Peacock name. Double marking was a common practice in the distribution centers which sold jewelry made by individual designers.

Shreve Company of California was another of these companies similar in nature.

In the Southwest, American Indian jewelry was being distributed. A vast amount of information exists regarding American Indian jewelry and is outside the scope of this chapter. However, it is doubtful that Art Nouveau had any impact.

The Art Nouveau movement in the United States, like in Europe, reached its peak at the turn of the century. It continued for the next five to ten years, but had died by the beginning of World War I. When the jewelry movement came back into existence in the United States, it was a completely new style. In the United States, the finest American jewelry, which paralleled the French jewelry of René Lalique, was produced at Tiffany & Co. in New York. No other American jeweler reached this level of workmanship.

XI
French Art Nouveau Jewelry

Paris was the nucleus of the Art Nouveau movement, and the style is at its purest when interpreted by French artists and craftsmen. In his contemporary commentary on French jewelry at the turn of the century, Gabriel Mourey says that the French have a special talent for producing articles of luxury.

> No unbiassed observer will deny the fact that with us there is more richness, more variety, more originality than can be found elsewhere; and the jewelry section in the Esplanade des Invalides at the Exhibition of 1900 showed to the whole world the progress made in this special branch of applied art by our craftsmen and our artists; showed, too, the verve, the imagination, the fancifulness, which are the special property of the French race in all that relates to articles of luxury, to those things which are essentially 'useless', if so we may term a woman's adornments.

While the Arts and Crafts movement was stirring in England, similar dissatisfaction was felt by artists all over France, with Gallé and the famous school in Nancy becoming a center for the new art and ideas. When Samuel Bing, a dealer in orientalia, rearranged his gallery in 1895 and renamed it L'Art Nouveau, artists from all over the world answered his call. He opened with an international exhibition in which artists from different countries contributed different aspects of applied and decorative arts. Each piece had to reflect the atmosphere and spirit of the age. Lalique showed jewelry there. The sound of Bing's simple name reverberated around the world, but the essence of the style, its exponents, and its ideology remained firmly centered in Paris.

At the Maison Moderne, another Paris gallery, director Meier-Graefe commissioned work from Dufrène, Follot, Orazzi, and Gaillard.

Lalique (1860–1945), more than any artist, epitomized French Art Nouveau jewelry. He was born in a small town on the River Marne and as a teenager showed a love and talent for sketching. He was apprenticed to the jeweler Louis Aucoc, studied at the Ecole des Arts Décoratifs, and probably spent time in an English Art School. Like nineteenth century jewelers, Lalique had started training as a young boy and had a thorough grounding in techniques and processes of nineteenth century jewelers' craft. Along with this, he had the imagination and the training of an artist, a new concept in the jewelry trade for we know that in the mid-nineteenth century designer-jewelers were rare. It was Lalique's rare combination of technical skill and artistic genius that resulted in the devastating beauty and quality of his Art Nouveau jewels.

The success of so many French Art Nouveau jewels and their obvious superiority in design, composition, and quality of manufacture and finish, is the product of this particular stage in French jewel history. Technical perfection had been the aim of French craftsmen throughout the century, with jewelers like Massin dedicated to the refinement of gem setting, and of what might be called "precision engineering." Specialization was an important aspect of rigorous training, and the French excelled in chasing

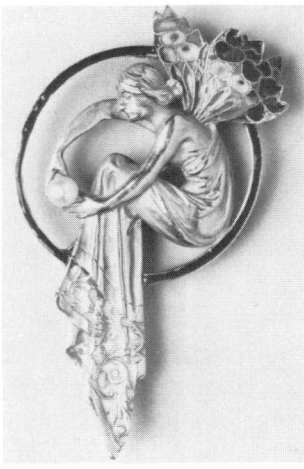

Plique à jour wings and gown with sculptured gold and enamel, by L. Masriere. The glistening white pearl is held so daintily it becomes the focus of attention. Note the workmanship in the folds of the draped gown.

33

goldwork, so that by the end of the nineteenth century, French jewels were characterized by the flow of soft goldwork, with the metal transformed almost into butter in the hands of the craftsmen. Also enameling techniques had been revived in the second half of the nineteenth century, particularly the open-backed *plique à jour*. Neo-Renaissance jewels of the 1870s and 1880s were richly adorned with enamelwork.

Opal and *plique à jour* enamel pendant with precious stones marked Leturcq.

Late nineteenth century jewelers had reaped the benefits of dedicated research, exploration, and refinement of techniques, and once the technical aspects had been absorbed new energies could be channelled into artistry which drew on the skills now at their disposal. It was a miracle of timing, of technical achievement, artistic struggles, changing social atmosphere, and the abandonment of the fin de siècle.

It is easy to forget that Lalique spent many years working on traditional nineteenth century French jewelry. When he returned to Paris from England, he worked for various jewelers including Cartier, Boucheron, and his master Aucoc. He continued to work on the premises he bought from Jules Destape in 1884. Later he moved to larger premises, and after 1890, in his atelier in the rue Thérèse, he began to experiment and explore his own fantasies in jewel design.

In 1895, his work reached the public when he exhibited for the first time at the Salon du Champs de Mars. His jewels received immediate acclaim and he went from strength to strength leading up to the highpoint of Art Nouveau at the Paris exposition of 1900. Here his most sensational pieces were on view.

Plique à jour pendant with diamonds and tourmalines that deepen in color as they descend the pendant. Paris mark without maker's mark.

It was Lalique who expressed a new, realistic view of nature through his jewels. He understood the process of nature, of death and rebirth—all symbolic of the death of the century and the beauty and implicit hopefulness of the birth of the new century. He had a true artist's eye for color and composition and was a master of surprises, mixing thick black geometric lines with the palest swirling enamels, mixing a dreamy nymph's face with the flaccid web of bat's wings, interpreting a deceptively classical cameo scene in deep, shocking colors of *pâte de verre*. The shock was always subtle, brilliantly composed. Flowers, insects, roosters, birds were given new life: petals splayed outwards in luscious fullness, carved of opaque glass; deep blue swallows dipped through the air, appropriately on a hair comb as well as a brooch; the spiky hardness of the pinecone or water plant thrust its way into being in the softest of pastel colors.

Lalique introduced movement, and especially pioneered the female nude figure after 1895. Lalique's ingenuity of design was balanced by his feeling and understanding of materials. One of the basic claustrophobic rules of nineteenth century jewelers that he set about breaking was associated with gemstones. he was never intimidated by their intrinsic value or, conversely, by their worthlessness. Like Giuliano, but more adventurous, he judged materials by their visual beauty, texture, color and their potential for adding to the composition and overall effect of his creations.

It is reputed to have been Lalique who introduced horn into jewelry. He was drawn to the cloudy translucency of horn, carving it into leaves and flowers, sometimes staining the material for added emphasis, such as an autumnal effect, or the luminous sheen of butterfly wings.

Lalique was master of enameling and of the *plique à jour* process, which he used to great effect to recreate the mesmerizing and tantalizing translucency of nature's shifting colors; to echo the changing tints of the opal—a favorite Art Nouveau stone; or to imply the changing subtleties of feminine erotic beauty. He also used opaque and matt enamels for intensity of color.

Glassworking was an important part of the whole movement, and Lalique joined this experimentation and incorporated opaque, carved glass, and *pâte de verre* (ground remolded glass) into his jewels. He never used new techniques self consciously, so that the onlooker is never immediately aware of the massive innovation of his work.

Lalique was commissioned by Gulbenkian, the wealthy industrialist, to make a series of spectacular jewels, now in Lisbon. After this, he was disillusioned and disgusted by the host of poor reproductions that his work had inspired, and he turned his attention more and more to glasswork. Later jewels consist of simple brooches and pendants hung on silk, all made of carved glass, still in his distinctive style.

Endless lists of French craftsmen were working in Paris in the Art Nouveau style at the turn of the century. French work is characterized by fine goldwork, subtle shaded enameling, by the freshness of the composition and the successful marriage of shape, motif, movement, and technique.

The house of Vever produced spectacular jewels and employed famous craftsmen, designers such as Grasset, enamelists, and engravers. It was a feature of French Art Nouveau that the best craftsmen worked at times for many different firms, and then sometimes alone. It was a very closed circle of artist and jewelers.

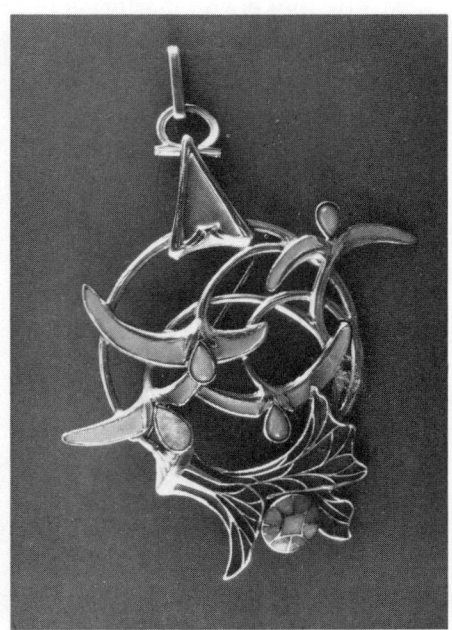

Gold enameled pendant signed G. Fouquet.

After Lalique, Fouquet and Vever, the most famous names associated with innovative and attractive work are probably Gaillard, Gautrait, and Descomps, but this has to be a subjective choice. Once again, Gaillard had been trained in the traditions of the nineteenth century craft, and his family had been jewelers for several generations. Following the pattern of specialization, Gaillard had been trained mainly as a silversmith. His Art Nouveau work shows the strong influence of Japanese art and design, which captivated the young jeweler around 1878. Gaillard produced many objects in the Japanese style, and became famous for working in horn, especially for organic-shaped hair ornaments such as sheafs of wheat, inspired by the work of his friend and colleague Lalique. Gaillard was also an expert enamelist and is known to have imported Japanese craftsmen to work in his atelier. Gautrait and Descomps were both immensely versatile and made fine use of the female head motif, the movement of insect wings, water nymphs, and sunsets.

Very little is known about the life and work of

most of the French workers; however, their stylistic range and consistently high standard of production identify French work as surely as any hallmark. It is interesting that so many makers appear to have made one or two superb pieces of jewelry, so that when handling their work you feel they must be major figures in the movement. And it is not unusual to come across a superb piece of French jewelry by an unheard-of maker, as if that single creative effort drained his emotional and artistic resources. This makes Lalique's prolific and consistent output all the more miraculous.

Enameled, sculptured gold, and gem-set dragonfly watch. Note the feeling of twisting and movement and the extension of the leaves beyond the borders of the watch.

Also, the nature of the artistic atmosphere meant that many more artists lent their hand to jewel design, perhaps for the first time, and such pieces would have been produced by a major or smaller firm of jewelers. The firm of Plisson and Hartz was outstanding in the production of excellent Art Nouveau jewelry. Many pieces of remarkable beauty and composition, with their mark, still appear in shops and auctions.

Other exceptional jewelers whose Art Nouveau pieces are still encountered include the following:

Lucien Gautrait did some work for the Vever Firm but worked chiefly for Gariod. He often signed his name on the reverse and made excellent Art Nouveau jewelry with heavy *plique à jour* enamel and beautiful sculptured gold.

Paul Lienard was a superb jeweler and designer using transparent and opaque enamels with unsurpassed skill. He utilized baroque pearls with startling effect.

Fernand Thesmar was one of the best enamelists of the period. His *plique à jour* enamels were masterpieces. He often used bright contrasting colors of striking beauty.

Paul and Henri Vever were leaders in Art Nouveau jewelry and used designs by Grasset and Colonna. Their work was somewhat heavier and more rigid than Lalique's. Henri Vever wrote a three volume history on nineteenth century jewelry.

Phillipe Wolfers from Brussels, Belgium was born in to a family of jewelers and made many Art Nouveau masterpieces. A large number were signed with his monogram *PW* in a shield and marked *"Exemplaire Unique"*. He was a master jeweler as well as a sculptor, anatomist, and botanist. He used baroque pearls with great effect and combined gold with *pique à jour* and opaque enamels along with carving in ivory. His works are comparable to Lalique's.

Edmond Becker worked for Boucheron and combined enameled gold with carved woods, making use of his training in wood sculpture.

Frederick Boucheron had a large firm and produced excellent Art Nouveau jewelry. His chief artists were L. Hirly and J. Brateau. The name "Cartier" appeared on the reverse of many pieces. Brateau also worked for Bapst.

Cartier made some pieces of Art Nouveau jewelry and generally stamped the firm name on the reverse. They also did some work with *plique à jour* enamels, but most of their emphasis was on classic jewelry and gemstones.

George De Riboucourt developed his own style of enameled gold jewelry in the Art Nouveau style.

Charles Desrosiers designed for Fouquet but his name does not appear on the jewelry.

Eugene Feuillatre was a leading enamelist and sculptor goldsmith working for several firms as well as for himself.

George Fouquet, next to Lalique, was the most accomplished Art Nouveau jeweler. He used many of Mucha's, Desrosier's, and Grosset's designs, and he introduced various spiked plants, thistles, and sinister insects in designing jewelry.

Finally, a peculiarly French feature of jewelry design was the botanical influence. The preoccupation with flowers and nature had made its way through the nineteenth century, and during the second Empire reached a height in terms of naturalism. The Japanese influence and new view of nature turned this naturalism into Art Nouveau, and irises, lilies, poppies, fuchsias, and orchids began to adorn jewels and works of art in the 1890s. So often taken as a sudden innovation belonging to the new art, this love of flowers, and especially of new species, sprung from a long French tradition. The emphasis at the turn of the century was on the more romantic and sensuous species, on symbolism and the realism of nature seen through the artist's eye.

Most of the pictures in this book are of French Art Nouveau pieces, and the commentaries describe the innovative features of design, composition, and material, as well as their beauty.

XII
Photographs and Captions

A variety of small Art Nouveau jewels are shown. The Madonna is by Hasé, and the small pendant above it is English. The others are French and American. Sycamore leaves are very common, especially in American jewelry.

Pendant signed G. Fouquet shows his ingenious ability to use thinly sliced opal in cloissons with enamels and gems.

An entrancing sunset scene on heavy gold signed by Plisson and Hartz. Note the workmanship, design, and use of subtle coloring.

Stained glass enameling is a striking technique used by only a few Art Nouveau jewelers. DeSuau was especially talented in this method. This large pendant contains a wedding medallion by Roty dated 1895. The silver framework bears an inscription dated 23 October 1901 and the name "de Forceville."

While not classically Art Nouveau, this floral spray (7 cm. long) on 15 ct. gold was made in 1896 to celebrate Queen Victoria's Jubilee. The brilliant iridescent enamels were developed specifically for this occasion and are called "Jubilee Enamel."

The *top left* brooch is of very heavy gold and made in France. From the female's head flow the long, winding tresses of hair that make up the entire brooch and intertwine with flowers, scattered diamonds, and turquoise. It portrays the eternal circle of life from beginning to end. The round brooch with three stones has no identifying marks, but is probably of English origin. The *lower left* brooch with plique à jour is signed Cartier. The *lower right* one with glass and enamel is by R. Lalique.

Three magnificent French Art Nouveau jewels. The large pendant with a carved ivory centerpiece is unsigned, but demonstrates a remarkable use of colored opaque and plique à jour enamels mixed with gems, flowers, and a pink pearl drop. The other two are by Joe Descomps, a master of plique à jour enameling and sculpturing in gold. Using a magnifier to study these pictures will reveal breathtaking beauty and detail.

Dog collar signed R. Lalique. Gold, enamel, and diamonds. The thick, subdued enameling with intertwined tendrils and eternal twisting are typical of Lalique's work. Movement and naturalism predominate.

The butterfly brooch and diamond dog collar are French, but no maker's marks are evident. The butterfly wings move and contain brilliant gems of the finest quality. The opals are split with diamond inserts. The plique à jour enamel is shaded with subtle transition. The dog collar is most unusual in its configuration, with a triangular diamond, pink plique à jour enamel, and glistening pearls.

Three Art Nouveau bracelets. The *top* one by Tiffany & Co. has brilliant fire opals in 18 ct. gold with scattered demantoid garnets. The sculptured gold setting is characteristic of Tiffany's swirling line work. The *middle* bracelet by Lalique has a large fire opal surrounded by sapphires and blue enameled leaves in each segment. The *lower* bracelet by Boucheron demonstrates brilliant sculpturing in heavy 18 ct. gold.

Lalique made both these pieces, using heavy enamels and sculptured gold for the *top* brooch; glass and enameled gold for the *bottom* hair comb. (The comb part fits into the base.) 9 cm. x 5 cm.

The basic design, workmanship, and material used for this pendant are characteristic of the jewelry of Phillipe Wolfers. Even though it is unmarked, similar pieces made by Wolfers can be found.

Pendant composed of gold, diamonds, opaque and translucent enamels. Inscribed LALIQUE. 6 cm. x 5.5 cm. The shimmering diamonds of the waterfall reflect the sunlight that bounces off the golden leaves at the top of this pendant. One senses the coolness of the shaded areas of the curving stream that culminates in cascades of diamonds in the waterfall. The two floating swans and the stream seem to convey a sense of gentle movement and peace and harmony. The shading of the enamel in the waterfall simulates water itself.

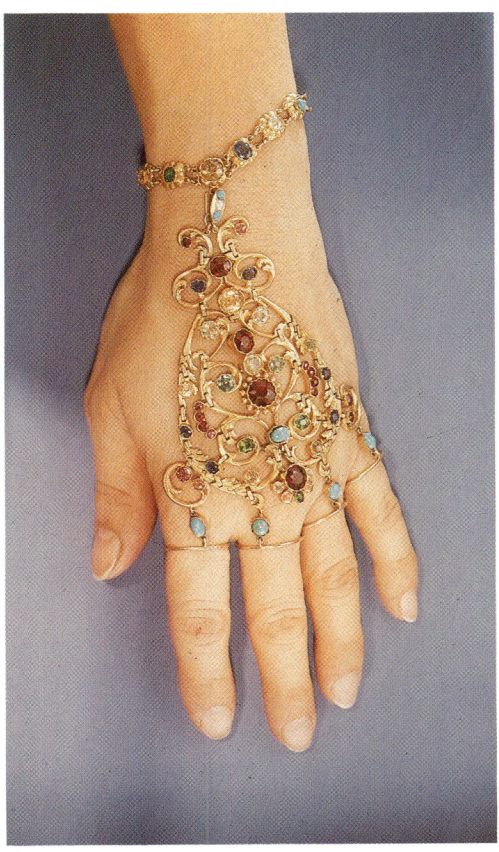

Handpiece signed Tiffany & Co. made of precious and semi-precious stones including demantoids, sapphires, turquoises, garnets, and rubies. Every joint is flexible.

Large pearl pendant with a cape of enameled gold and diamonds topped with an enameled flower. Stamped F.M. (probably Froment-Meurice). 5 cm.

An unsigned French dragonfly brooch with plique à jour shaded enamel wings and fire opal hindwings. The body has diamond inserts and eyes of demantoid garnets. The wings are not mobile. 7 cm. x 5 cm.

Spectacle case of 14 ct. gold, enamel, rubies, and opals. Signed Marcus Co. width 10 cm. While not strictly a piece of jewelry, this spectacle case is typical of what one has come to expect of Art Nouveau. Four bands of bluish green enamel curve to the edge of the case, but do not continue on the underside. The outer two bands have large rubies set in a mound of gold surrounded by arcs of enamel. Each of the two inner bands is broken by an irregularly shaped ruby; two large elongated opals are in the center of the case. The wavy, flowing pattern and the mixture of bright colors emphasize the Art Nouveau aspects of this case; however it is purely decorative and lacks the emotional substance and sensitivity of true Art Nouveau masterpieces.

Moth signed P.W. (P. Wolfers). Wings 11.7 cm.; body 7.5 cm.; width 3.75 cm. Composed of 18 ct. gold, translucent and opaque enamel, rubies, diamonds, and pearls. Made in Belgium. The colors in this enchanting moth blend so subtly that one cannot see where one shade begins and the other ends. Even in artificial light, the vivid colorations and sheen of jeweled enamel and gold seem to sparkle in the sunlight. The flaming orange enamel in the lower wing is spectacular. It appears as if the diffraction spectrum of the rubies on the edge of the upper wing has been simulated in the lower wing, making it seem as though sunlight is being transmitted downward. This is a unique innovation in jewelry. This is also a superb example of cloisonné enamel with plique à jour technique. Note the remarkable reticular formation of the goldwork and the shaded enamels to melt through the compartments. Two oval mounds of meticulously faceted rubies, pierced by a gold prong set in silver veins, spot the wings. Small rubies form the eyes. Jeweled tentacles and diamonds on the ribbed body trail down into a thin abdomen of matched pearls ending in a small curved jeweled claw. Gold ribs seen translucently through the life-like enamel make the veins in the wings, while the reverse of the piece shows the golden reticular architecture that solidifies the delicate hues of the flying insect.

Gold and diamond brooch with plique à jour and opaque enamels signed Lalique. Paris, ca. 1903. (Dating is based on a similar brooch purchased in 1904 from the Louisiana Purchase Exposition, now in the Walters Art Gallery, Baltimore.) Height 4 cm.; width 7 cm. A subtle, mystical ecstasy exudes from the beautifully sculptured gold female in this brooch. Her long, flowing tresses are typical of those found in many female figures depicted in the Art Nouveau manner. The sinewy curves of the background both extend the artistic dimensions and add a completeness of design to the brooch. Small glistening diamonds and deep blue enamel (simulating sapphires) blend harmoniously with the pastel enamel of varying colors. Freedom and boldness are in abundance and the piece itself superbly portrays the beauty, warmth, and grace personifying the "Art Nouveau woman."

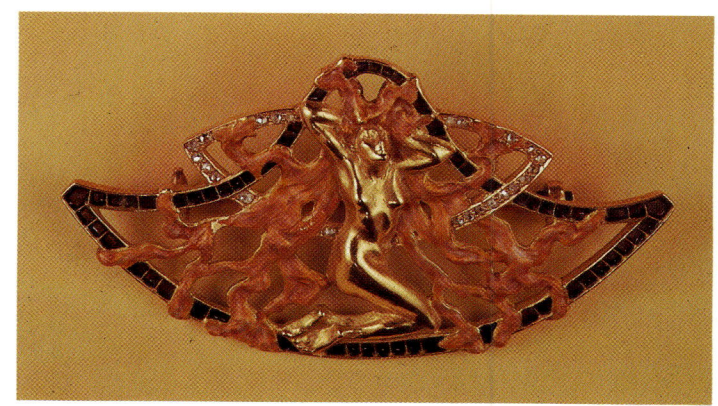

Orchid of 18 ct. gold, translucent enamel, pearls, and diamonds. Signed G. Fouquet. Paris. Height 7.5 cm.; width 10 cm. A huge pearl the size and shape of a walnut comprises the body of the orchid. The pearl is veined and flesh-colored to resemble an anatomic specimen that may well have reminded Fouquet that the orchid flower was named by the ancients because of its resemblance to the male gonad. This strange artifact and the pale, washed green enamel that ties the flower together make this fantastic orchid a unique masterpiece. The flower leaves of gold and translucent enamel curved and spread like a jack-in-the-pulpit. The broad gold-veined lip and life-like petals are surmounted by a large iridescent pink pearl in a crown from which stamens and pistils of round and elongated pears stand forth. Deep purple enamel held by gold strips form the veins in the flower's petal, and the strange large pearl at the base is entrapped in a curving network of enameled gold bands. Diamonds of different sizes stud all parts of the unusual flower. Softness, grace, and sparkling beauty are the chief features of this impressionistic delight.

In all likelihood this orchid made history in July 1963 at Christie's art auction, the oldest in the world. Hughes describes the event as follows: "But this was probably the first time a truly modern jewel has ever been sold second-hand for more than the cost of its mineral content. A sixty-year old masterpiece by Georges Fouquet which, if melted, might produce £430, actually fetched £420. The odd £390 were paid for the inspired shape of this four inch enamelled orchid. The oft repeated but cynical claim that true value is melting value is at last proved wrong. The artist does matter: his impact on jewels is now apparent to the accountant as well as the aesthete."

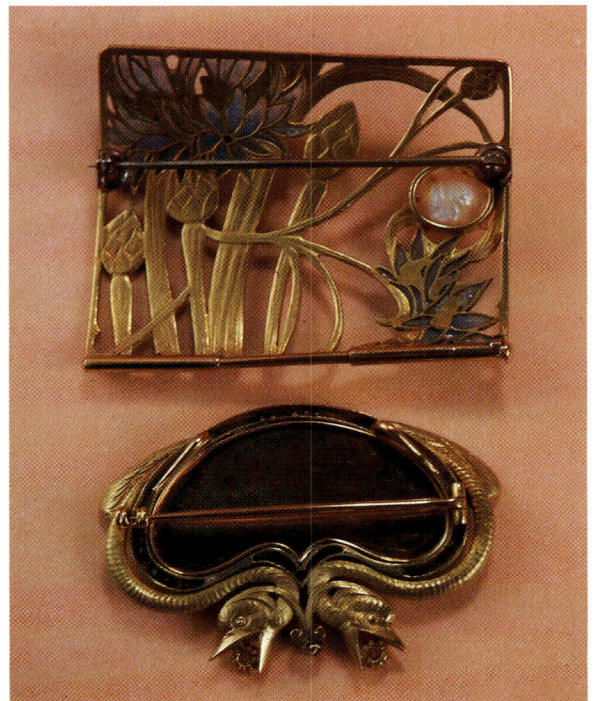

The green and purple brooch, *above,* demonstrates a most unusual example of French Art Nouveau enameling. It is very thick, with unusual color contrast, and is particularly heavy around the edges. The goldwork is also extraordinarily solid and very heavy. The excellent finish on the reverse of this brooch is shown in the figure *below,* and in addition, there is shown the reverse of a section of jewelry made by Lalique which also demonstrates the care given to the entire piece when made by a master. Detailed handwork is evident in all good pieces, both on the front and on the reverse. The purple brooch unfortunately is not signed.

Dragonfly pendant. Monogrammed on the counter-enamel, Fernand Thesmar. France, ca. 1900. 8.6 cm. x 5.4 cm. Gold and enamel dragonfly perched on a trilium leaf with a deep green enamel background. Gold veins mark the leaf and the wings of the dragonfly. The brilliant enamel is bold to a unique degree. Thesmar made few pieces of jewelry and this one shows his remarkable competence for combining color, space, and design into a piece of art. The Japanese influence is most evident in this dragonfly.

Village brooch of enameled gold and diamonds. Signed R. Lalique. This is a rare example of Lalique's work with extraordinarily thin plique à jour enamel. The village scene is of the sheerest enamel, and the perspective is obtained with inlaid, waving, thin gold wire and an almost imperceptible shading of color which changes dramatically in different light sources. The triangular diamond drop is a replacement of the original curved pear-shaped drop which was much more consistent with Art Nouveau lines.

Pendant of gold, diamonds, opals, pearls, and translucent cabochon enamel. Inscribed Cte Du Suau de la Croix. Height 8.7 cm.; width 6.5 cm. The cabochon is made to simulate amethysts and emeralds. The pearls, diamonds, and opals are real, but all of the rest is enameling of a most unusual and innovative style distinctive to this artist. He worked mostly with silver, but this piece blends gold and silver in a tasteful manner.

Large gold watch with plique à jour enameled face and case. Signed Lalique. French, 1901. 6.4 cm. x 7.6 cm. The case is covered with orange, gray and pale green enameled carnation petals waving rhythmically in a tantalizing erotic motion. The flower seems to disappear into space off the edges of the curved surface, extending the viewer's imagination.

An example of a "put together" brooch. The central part with the lovely female and flowers is Art Nouveau. The outer frame is Victorian. Inspection of the reverse shows the cold solder areas where the two parts were put together. Study the differences between the two parts.

Necklace. A. Auger. Paris, ca. 1905. 7.6 cm. x 8.9 cm. A large necklace in the Egyptian motif. Two graceful sphinxes carved of pure white opals gaze at the Egyptian scarab of chrysoprase set with gold, diamonds, and emeralds. The wings are of a deep blue and green enamel. Diamond-studded flowers and small emeralds in wavy network support the scarab and sphinxes. Small cut emeralds look like eyes to give the base the semblance of a mask. The necklace is startling and dramatic.

Rings. *Top row:* all are Art Nouveau by makers like Lalique, Fouquet, Marcus, and Rambour. *Second row:* the ring with blue enamel and a circle of pearls is from the early 19th century, and the ruby snake ring is also not Art Nouveau. The ring on the left is by G. Fouquet. *Third row:* Lalique made the first ring, but the small opal ring is early 19th century and the big oval gold ring is in the style of Castellani. The rest are Art Nouveau. *Fourth row:* the scarab ring is by Lalique. The snake ring is Victorian and the rough cut diamond ring is 18th century. *Fifth row:* the second ring, of faceted jade and diamonds is certainly not Art Nouveau. The large opal cameo ring and the emerald and diamond ring are also not Art Nouveau. *Bottom row:* the first ring is Chinese jade and 24 ct. gold, the next is opal in a Victorian setting, the third is an English memorial ring, the fourth is Chinese jade, and the next two are Victorian. None is in the Art Nouveau style in this row. These rings clearly demonstrate differences between Art Nouveau and some of the other periods.

A variety of Art Nouveau pins and pendants. The proud peacock is unmarked. The wavy water scene with ducks is marked by Joe Descomps. The plique à jour pendant with moving swans is by Lalique. The impressionistic painting (*lower left*) is by the talented English goldsmith Phoebe Traquair. The intricate enameled pendant (*lower right*) is typical of the French goldsmith DeRibeaucourt. The plique à jour Madonna pendants are by Cashira-Y-Carreras. The plique pendant with the peridot at the base has illegible marks. Despite the differences in all of these, they still show the basic features of Art Nouveau.

Pendant of gold and plique à jour enamel. Signed G. Fouquet. The perspective in this plique à jour pendant is achieved by wavy gold lines outlining clouds, hills, water, and sky. The bold projecting trees in sculptured 18 ct. gold are a notable innovation in jewelry. The deep background extends the artistic dimensions yet gives a sense of unity to the entire brooch. The piece would be incomplete without the pink baroque pearl that glistens like a distant sun. A sensation of airiness, freshness, and outdoor fragrance seems to emanate from this delightful scene. The pendant itself is almost as light as a feather.

Brooch marked Lalique. 6 cm. x 5.5 cm. A carnation of blended pink and white opalescent glass. By varying the thickness of the glass a subtle shading is produced. Behind is a leaf of greenish blue translucent enamel honeycombed with gold veins. Two large fire opals blend into a background of gold leaves with burnished enamel on gold. The reverse of this brooch is elaborately designed with a hydrangea blossom of bluish opaline glass. The entire jewel is a blending of soft and subdued blues, greens, and white with a remarkable balance and unity. The brooch was in all likelihood designed more as an artistic masterpiece than as jewelry to be worn. Its use of sculptured glass, jewels, and enamel shows Lalique at his best. After his early years, Lalique deserted bright sparkling colors for the subtler shades and delicate harmonies evident in this brooch.

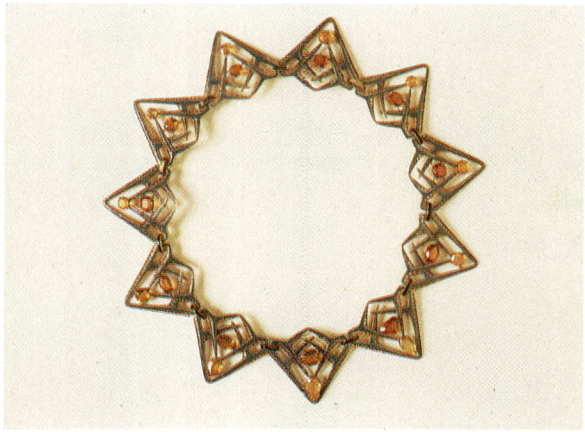

Necklace stamped Lalique. An early work by Lalique using geometric, spiky rhomboids enameled with sage green and set with light and dark faceted topaz. The edges are set with tiny half pearls that add a subtle softness to this rather mournful and almost unique design for Lalique. It was probably made before he immersed himself into the organic flow of Art Nouveau.

All these pieces were made in Russia and stamped with marks of Fabergé workmasters. Note the characteristic flowing curves of Art Nouveau. The bar brooch *(top)* probably celebrates a tenth anniversary. Rubies were not ordinarily supposed to be used for royal pieces, since the Tsarevitch had hemophilia and red rubies were avoided because of the connotation. The man's watch pendant *(left)* celebrates an important Romanoff event in 1651 during the reign of Alexei Mikhailovitch, the second Romanoff czar. The front and back flaps lift up to reveal a list of illustrious Romanoff names. The two white enamel pendants are typical of Fabergé's work. The one with diamonds has a guilloche background. The pendant to the right of the Romanoff locket has light green garnets called demantoids that are found chiefly in Russia and are considered rare stones. The intricate brooch *(bottom)* with enameled sycamore leaves is sprinkled with small poorly cut diamonds, rubies, and chrysoprase. Fabergé set his diamonds in a characteristic cup which is evident in all these pieces. Practically all Russian lockets are so well made they are airtight and close with a "thud."

Brooch by Paul Lienard. France. Gold, baroque pearls, semi-opaque and translucent enamels. 11.5 cm. x 9 cm. With fluttering wings, the bees gently grasp glistening silver and white pearls on the wisteria frond. The cascade of pearls is on movable stems and shimmers with motion. The opaque, luminous enameled bees glisten as though reflecting sunlight. Note the variation and gradation of colors in each segment of the enameled wings. The eyes and heads of the bees are both fascinating and startling to the viewer.

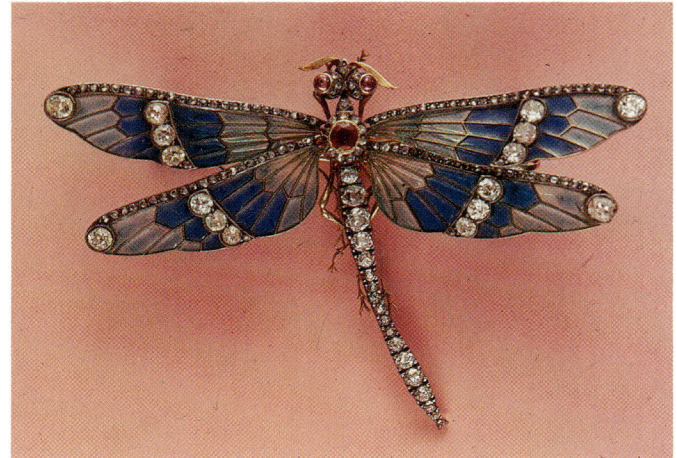

The dragonfly was a commonly used insect in Art Nouveau jewelry. In this instance, the shaded and uniform enameling is extraordinary and inset with diamonds, a very difficult technique. The wings move, and the body of diamonds and head of rubies present a magnificent spectacle when seen under various light sources.

Most of the these pieces are Art Nouveau. The most obvious Victorian piece is the cameo pendant to the *left* on the *third row* down. The small gold and hardstone egg just below this actually looks like Art Nouveau, but it is of the 18th century in the Rococo style. The enameled griffin next to the egg is by Fanniere Frères and is pre-Art Nouveau in the Renaissance Revival style. In the *top row,* the crowned woman pendant with pearls is also of Victorian period and not of Art Nouveau. Six pieces have plique à jour enamel. Can you identify them? The large enameled butterfly uses translucent enamel, and the green watch and pink enameled female face to the *right* on the *third row* use opaque enamels painted on a gold base.

This unusual French brooch signed V.R. consists of glass with enameled and gold inlays surrounded by bamboo twigs. It represents a natural whirlpool. The central opal matrix, when stared upon, has a peculiar sheen, and if gazed upon long enough creates an hypnotic effect of the whirlpool going round and round. This was probably the first time such a concept was introduced into a three-dimensional jeweled object.

Stylized and extraordinary flower pin. Signed V.R., an unrecorded goldsmith. The brilliant enameling is somewhat unusual, as is the shape of this peculiar but handsome pin.

A very subdued colored enameled brooch on 18 ct. gold. Unsigned but probably by Plisson and Hartz. The shaded opaque enamel is in the best Art Nouveau manner.

Watches. The two flowered watches are Art Nouveau. The miniature one (*left*) has soft colors blending into each other, gentle curves, and no sharp angles. The green watch (*middle*) shows the flowing lines and stylized female, with her semi-erotic face and flowing hair, so characteristic of Art Nouveau. The black and white watch is in Art Deco style, showing clearly the contrasting sharp colors of black and white enamels, geometric angles, and straight lines.

This lovely dragonfly brooch is composed of gold horn, precious stones, and enamels. It is stamped with the maker's mark L. Aucoc. France. 12.5 cm. x 6.5 cm. Utilizing a difficult technique of simulating cabochon jewels with mounds of built-up enamels, the artist has created a unique dragonfly. Gold horn is used in an especially effective way to achieve the firm wings upon which the enamels and gems are placed. The coloring is subtle yet rich and daring. The Japanese influence is evident in the designer's use of attachments, legs, and color contrasts. Note the unusual curves in the body and in the tail of the insect and the flowing changes of color in the enameling. This dragonfly was probably made by Lalique when he worked for the Aucoc firm.

Man's stickpin. Women were idealized and used as a principal motif for Art Nouveau jewelry and practically all of the jewelry was made for female adornment. Comparatively few pieces were made for men. Stickpins and cravat pins are the exceptions, although some men's rings and watch chains were also created. Stickpins of the period are often works of art in miniature. This stick pin shows the use of a demonic figure in plique à jour enamel. Many thousands of Art Nouveau stickpins still exist and many are excellent art objects displaying the ingenuity of the enamelists and goldsmiths.

These watches demonstrate some of the excellent techniques of the Art Nouveau goldsmiths. They are all French except for the long one with sapphires and swirling goldwork made by Marcus & Co. The others show the remarkable beauty achieved with plique à jour and opaque enamels combined with sculptured gold and a delicate use of gems.

Bleeding heart necklace by L. Gaillard. Masterful pink enameling with a swirling, shaded opalescence and very thick enamels. The pink flowers express the sensuality of nature and contrast brilliantly with the more traditional and naturalistic goldwork, which is extremely finely chased. This is an important illustration of the development of Art Nouveau from 19th century naturalism and from the French speciality of chasing and working gold. The beautifully colored plump and hanging heart-shaped flowers were very poplar motifs on several Art Nouveau jewels. Here the flowers are surrounded by entwined boughs and leaves.

Caldwell necklace. This striking Arts & Crafts style necklace was influenced by English forms and colors. The opals and enamels appear to be a diversion for the traditional firm of J. E. Caldwell; the lights in the opals are emphasized by the deep green and blue blended enamels. Movement here is more controlled and the design more abstract with heavier sweeps of color that change and mingle.

Lalique necklace. The overall impression of the softest pastel colors comes from the amber glass cut into organic plant motifs which offset the brilliance of the stones and the warm luster of the pearls, similarly, the curves contrast and soften the spiky movement of each unusual plant motif.

Gold pendant in the distinctive manner of Van Strydonck. Displays the more vigorous and angular movement of the whiplash Art Nouveau line, softened with leaves of diamonds, pearls, and a single ruby, the drop encased on this occasion within the finely textured gold framework.

Lalique swallows brooch. Signed R. Lalique. 8.5 cm. x 5 cm. Movement is the essence of this brooch by Lalique. The two soaring, deep blue swallows hold in their beaks slender diamond-tipped branches skimming backwards in the wind as the tapering outstretched wings of the birds cut a swift swirling flightpath through the air. The birds and their feathered wings are enameled on gold in light and dark blue, with the Lalique quality of goldwork seen on the feather-textured back of the jewel. Lalique has created an impression of speed incorporating the soaring Art Nouveau line as the very trailing branches meet the birds' tails forming a wonderful composition. The unique sense of freedom and boldness make this an outstanding work of art.

Lalique rooster brooch. 5.5 cm. x 9 cm. A breathtaking combination of action and color as the proud golden rooster, meticulously sculpted in the richest of goldwork, pecks intently at the pool of swirling pale enamels, the full, feathered tail sweeping upwards towards the sky. Note again the clever composition with the natural swirling of the tail feathers lending the touch of Art Nouveau sensuality. The pool below is of pale pastel and white-tinged enamels with contrasting heavier black angular lines. The great sincerity and strength evident in the sculpture is reminiscent of Picasso. Note the remarkable perspective obtained with color, line, and angle.

a) The best jewels with female motifs show very intense expressions on the face, with finely molded features. This exquisitely sculpted heart-shaped face is tilted high inquiringly. The softly waving hair is lost in curling foliage in which nestle three peacock's feathers. The brooch is centered with emeralds and diamonds and has a long dog's tooth pearl drop. b) This mysterious carved profile is tilted even higher and was perhaps the first time a woman's face had been depicted in this erotic fashion. The cleverly chosen flesh-colored pâte de verre is temptingly tilted and the eyes closed in ecstasy within Lalique's fine goldwork frame. The hair adds to the shape of the head and the total composition; tied loosely at the back, it hangs down her neck leading the eye toward the single diamond and pearl. The softly moving gold frame is further set with diamonds. c) This total celebration of femininity and sensuality is a colorfully enameled brooch that bears the initials H. G. in a style like that of Hector Guimard, although this designer is not known to have made or designed jewelry. The female form can be seen clearly beneath the exciting swirl of skirts in shaded plique à jour enamels of opal, pink, blue, and lavender rimmed with diamonds. Her arms are folded back seductively behind her head and she rests in a recess of green plique à jour enamel edged with red and set with diamonds. This vision of swirling skirts was a reflection of the current popularity of Loine Fuller, who caused a sensation with her free dancing and use of swirling fabrics.

Gold pendant. Unsigned but attributed to Zorra. 6 cm. x 8 cm. The female head and loose hair are sculpted in gold that moves as freely as the water that holds her peaceful dreamy gaze. Loose spreading hair falls over and around the shoulders to form the fluid outline for the calm pool of blue plique à jour enamel; off center floats one lily pad in veined matte green enamel. The new image of dreamy femininity is further expressed by the pink opalescent enameled flowers with glints of gold in her hair and balanced below in the center with one flowers with glints of gold in her hair and balanced below in the center with one flowerhead, again off center, in keeping with the current fashion for lack of symmetry. The tiny opal in the center of the forehead echoes the colors of the enamels and was a popular feature in female motifs.

The opal was a favorite stone with Art Nouveau jewelers and one that was particularly appropriate in female themes for its soft colors that change subtly with each glance. The heavy formal French gold framework carries an erotic naked nymph perched on one side, with folds of fabric rustling about her, her head thrown back, and her hair flying. Below the central opal, ferns spread into the most typical of all Art Nouveau motifs: a display of deep blue and green plique à jour peacock's feathers set with diamonds.

Unusual pendant by Lalique using the classical female form. A dancing nymph with draped diaphanous robes holding a garland of floating flowers, cleverly interpreted in pâte de verre. The soft lilac background contrasts shockingly with the dense vivid green in an unusually simple, classical gold frame. The more subtle statement of Art Nouveau comes from its contrasting colors and slightly irregular shape, together with the freedom and sensuality of the imprisoned dancing nymph. Again, like a symbol of the changing moods of femininity, the opal is embedded above the girl's head.

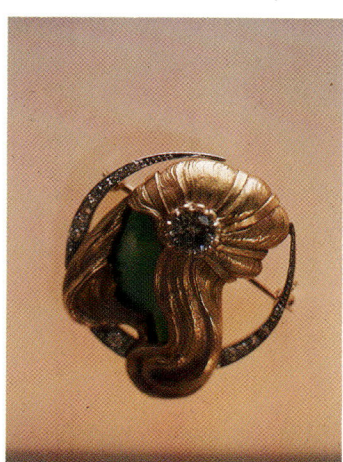

Brooch in the style of Bing with green pâte de verre aristocratic face in profile. The color adds another air of mystery to this female image. The goldwork has a particular luster and softness and the wild locks of hair are caught up with the diamond and framed in a crescent of diamonds celebrating the female as a mysterious goddess of the moon.

Three sisters by Boucheron in gold, enamel, and diamonds with a briolette peridot drop. Movement and life are emphasized in the chased and sculpted threesome of whimsical female heads, each carrying a different expression. Their flowing hair is transformed into naturalistic branches combining once again the themes of nature and femininity. Green enameled leaves reach the girl's heads and one single red flower sits in the middle of the group. The central figure wears a diamond necklace.

Gold-winged birds. The diamond-rimmed wings are outstretched to show feathers of pastel plique à jour enamels shading from lavender to pink and the palest of blue on an opalescent-enameled body and pearl-set head. A diamond drop hangs from the bird's long beak; it holds a ruby in its claws. Unsigned, but the back is inscribed: Pierre 25 Juillet 1904.

Two insects. Lalique saw insects with an unprecedented realism, transforming them at times into mythical creatures or just drawing out and emphasizing their natural beauty and miraculous anatomy. *Above*, the wings are enameled with plique à jour in varied shades of gold-flecked blues and lavenders very like the colors of opals. The upper section of the body is in gold and white enamel with brown stripes set with a pearl. The lower part is formed of a baroque pearl framed by enamel green and black spikes with extra hints of turquoise and rust colors: the famous juxtaposition of surprising colors. A single diamond fits between the black antenna. *Below*, one of the most successful versions of the popular winged female motif. Inspired by Loiie Fuller, this half-woman half-butterfly expresses the concept of female sensuality. The fabric swirled around the body shows the outline of the female form, while her outstretched arms cling to the opaque pastel-colored and diamond-set wings. The top wings are shaded from pink to green edges. Below the colors are deeper, and purple fades into blue. Generally these colors are brighter, more dense and opaque than on most butterfly wings.

Group of three demonic figures in late 19th century French tradition adapted to the Art Nouveau style. The *center* example, by Plisson and Hartz, uses plique à jour pale green enamel for outstretched wings with red tourmaline and diamond eyes. *Left*, a heavy gold watch with the griffin's outstretched wings feathered in green and red enamel. The same motif is adapted to the shape of the watch case below. Both figures are centered with diamond-set fleurs-de-lis. *Right*, by Fanniere Brothers, a subtle colored gold and oxidized silver piece featuring the entwined, rising bodies of three scaly and threatening monsters with ruby eyes, set with three pieces of lapis lazuli. Grotesque, whimsical, and ludicrous figures that both shocked and entertained were symbolic features of much Art Nouveau.

Group of dragonflies. The dragonfly, along with the peacock plume and erotic female, became a symbol of Art Nouveau jewelry. With its outstretched, gossamer-light, fluttering wings of ever-changing colors, variations were endless, and each artist interpreted the dragonfly in his own way according to his own fantasy, technical ambitions, and artistic skills. The dragonfly expressed the Art Nouveau preoccupation with nature, with dreamlike themes, vitality, and movement; it also provided a vehicle for the use of new materials, enamels, and techniques. Wings were often set *en tremblant* to add to the magic of these works of art. The colors were usually exceptionally subtle, transparent, and shaded, while lithesome bodies were often gem-set. The head and bodies could also show more depth of color with the use of rich enamel or lines of diamonds or colored stones. The Child and Child example is an unusual piece for this English firm, with a very thick-layered, deep, vibrant pink enamel contrasting the pale, thin, and subtle shading of green plique à jour wings. The blue dragonfly is by Alphonse Auger, Paris, with hovering wings and the most subtle shadowing of wing markings. The diamonds are set skillfully in the thinnest of plique à jour enamel. The slithering tail of sapphires leads from the rich cabochon sapphire body.

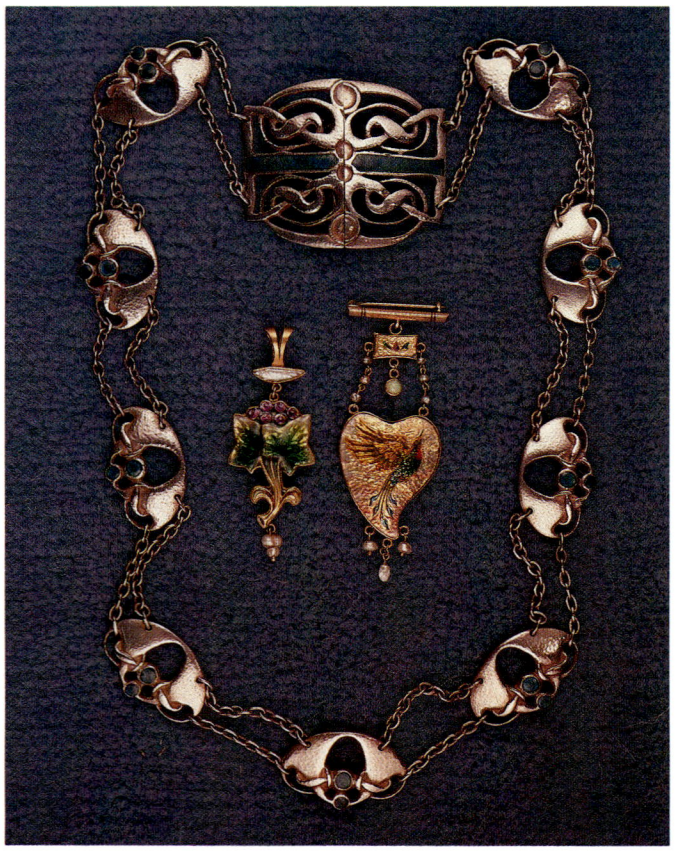

Liberty represented the English branch of Art Nouveau and introduced a late 19th century Celtic revival which had an affinity with the free-moving lines of Art Nouveau. Their main designer was Archibald Knox, who probably designed this hammered silver and floating blue green enamel belt made by Liberty & Co. Enameling was one of the most important aspects of the English Arts & Crafts movement and the foiled, highly opalescent enamel on the two pendants, center, is typical of the work of J. Cromer Watt, a Scottish jeweler. It is also representative of the progress made in enameling at this period and was one of the successes of Arts & Crafts. On the *left* is a vine and grape motif. On the *right*, a brooch in the form of a curved heart with soaring, colorful birds. Both feature the typical little pendant pearls.

Henry Wilson tiara. Henry Wilson was one of the most professional and successful Arts & Crafts designers. This tiara shows his highly individual use of leaves, which is one important way of distinguishing different Arts & Crafts designers, and the leaf theme continues in the enamelwork. The Gothic style outline is enhanced by rich medieval enamels. Wilson has also moved outside the general Arts & Crafts principles by adding small sapphires, diamonds, and a citrine to this creation.

Necklace and pendant in the style of Cromer Watt, master of this brilliant foiled and shaded enamelwork. The curved heart has added movement, another important characteristic of his work. Note also the depth of color and the brightness of the silvery tints together with the wrinkled, crumpled texture of the thick layers of distinctive enamelwork.

Arts & Crafts pieces by Child and Child, known as an Edwardian traditional jewelry firm working around the turn of the century. Enameling was a specialty of the firm. Their enamels were sometimes a little rough or unrefined, but always dramatic, deeply colored, effective, and highly distinctive. They specialized in a feathered wing motif, as in the green bird pendant (*top right*); and they are also known for their own very special bright blue enamelwork, as seen in the center of the brooch (*lower right*), here in the form of guilloche enamel. The two pendants (*left*) show Child and Child in revival mood, still using enamels in a medieval pastiche (*top*) and an 18th century style (*below*).

Collection of orchids. the most sensuous, luxurious flower of all, the exotic orchid was immortalized by Art Nouveau jewelers; its secretive crevices, the curls and twists of its petals, rich in velvety textures and dramatic coloring, all in suspended motion, delighted turn-of-the-century craftsmen. Tiffany made a specialty of reproducing in great detail the various species, using the widest range of enameling techniques developed at this stage, with gemset, encrusted centers and stems. A, B, C, and D are all Tiffany orchids made about 1890. Three are signed; the yellow one, unsigned.

A. 6.75 cm. x 6 cm. This uses the most dramatic dark enamels of all. Note the diamond-edged velvet 'tongue' and black markings on the outer leaves.

B. 9 cm. x 7 cm. A very large example, with deep contrasts in its mottled red and black, wrinkled petals, with their yellow edges, and the surprising brightness of the white edged center.

C. A softer version in shaded lilac with curling petals. A very elegant example with white marked center.

D. The blood red center is echoed by the line of rubies on the stem; and the pale, white-edged, lilac-veined petals curl more closely on this example around the exotic diamondset center.

Both E and F are in the manner of Tiffany, but are unsigned. Showing additional, very different species, they demonstrate the great attention to detail in enameling, capturing the exact colors of the flowers and the personality and beauty of each variety, from the soft lilac speckles mixed with amethysts and diamonds to the most vibrant yellow and red with a ruby stem and dramatic single diamond center.

Dragonfly brooch of enameled 18 ct. gold with diamonds and rubies. Signed Plisson and Hartz. 6 cm. x 5 cm. A superb example of a daring technique that uses irregular design and unstructured lines combined with nature in abstract. The soft colors and gentle flowers blend with the translucent dragonfly that seems to hover at a distance. Light colored plique à jour enamels simulate the gossamer wings of the insect as it prepares to dip into the pollen-ladened, sun-drenched flowers.

Angel brooch of 18 ct. gold, enamel, and diamonds. Signed L. Masriera. Portugal. 6.5 cm. x 4 cm. This golden angel is typical of the Art Nouveau female. Her long tresses seem to be blown by the wind as she alights on earth. Her head is bent forward and her mystical eyelids are slightly lowered, perhaps to behold the brilliant diamond below. The outstretched arms are graceful and so finely detailed that the muscles and tendons appear as shadows and hillocks in the flesh. Her sheer toga is shaded in its folds and slightly more translucent over her left breast and abdomen, suggesting a purity and subtleness that delights the observer. Her lowered wings and eyes and the flowing toga culminate in the diamond at the tip of the piece. The figure itself is encased in a heart of gold and diamonds, as if a halo glistened all around her.

Comb. Signed Lalique. The top is 8.9 cm. x 6.3 cm., made of 18 ct. gold with graduated sapphires and translucent and opaque enamels. The four teeth, made of horn, are 10.2 cm. long. This majestic comb reveals many of Lalique's talents but fails to display his genius for sculpturing glass, horn, gold, and ivory. Both sides of the comb are worked with equal care in a manner characteristic of Lalique. The comb's top is formed by one-and-a-half turns of two branches of engraved gold. The space between the branches is partially filled with half leaves of delightful blue translucent enamel in which fine gold veins twist and turn. Growing outward from the outer branch are triangular fresh young leaves edged and veined in gold delicately worked. The leaves are of opaque blue enamel so distinctly Lalique: the enamel varies in thickness, gloss, and shading. Lalique's handling of materials shows the influence of Gauguin's advice, "Do not finish your work too much."

Between each triangular leaf an oval sapphire fruit grows from a stem. The sapphires vary in shade and depth to harmonize with the adjoining leaves. And the leaves not only grow smaller and more delicate as they curve toward the end of the branch, but the deep blue enamel of the larger leaves gradually blends into subtle shades of blues and greens until the last small leaf fades into a delicate sea green in deference to a very light, greenish blue sapphire. Leaves and sapphires appear purplish when held up to artificial light and deep blue in sunlight. And through all of this, one perceives a sense of subtle motion. The beauty is breathtaking. This is Lalique: sensitive creator of harmony in color, material, form, and depth. He brought sunlight, emotion, and freedom that tradition had denied.

XIII
International Jewelers and Marks Circa 1900

American Jewelers and Marks Circa 1900

United States standards required the carat mark to be stamped on gold jewelry, and "sterling" or other designation on silver. Platinum and other precious metals also had their own designations. The gold used commonly for American jewelry was 10, 14, or 18 carat. Some jewelers of the period also stamped their names or marks on many pieces. Actually, only a few American firms produced Art Nouveau style jewelry and still fewer produced really artistic pieces. Tiffany and Co. was outstanding. They produced excellent Art Nouveau jewelry, including many masterpieces such as the orchids (Figure 8), but generally their jewelry was somewhat heavier, busier, and less subtle than French pieces. Marcus & Co. also produced outstanding Art Nouveau pieces, but with less artistry than Tiffany. Both firms were inclined to emphasize precious stones, although Marcus & Co. made unusual use of natural defects in precious and semi-precious stones and also created a characteristic style of enameling. Kohn & Krementz in Newark also made excellent pieces of Art Nouveau jewelry emphasizing sculptured gold and enamels. Florence Koehler was one of the few American jewelers who demonstrated expertise in the Arts and Crafts style.

The outstanding American firms that produced jewelry in the Art Nouveau style included Tiffany, Marcus, Kohn, Gorham, Krementz, Blank, Alling, Battin, Durand, Hedges, Kerr, Riker, Rogers, Spaulding, Walton, Whiteside, and Ballou. A few firms like Caldwell and Peacock occasionally sold Art Nouveau jewelry. Most American firms however emphasized traditional jewelry styles and the use of precious and semi-precious stones with little attention to enamling or artistic innovation.

JEWELRY MARKS

Reproduced, with additions, from *Trade Marks of Jewelers and Kindred Trades*, published 1896 by Jeweler's Circular Publishing Company, with permission from Jeweler's Circular Keystone (Radnor, Pennsylvania).

ABEL BROS. & CO.,
64-66 John St.,
NEW YORK.

ALLING & CO.,
180 Broadway,
NEW YORK.

(On Cards.)

A. & A.

(Discontinued.)

M. J. AVERBECK,
19 Maiden Lane,
NEW YORK.

T. W. A.

THOMAS W. ADAMS & CO.,
11 John St.,
NEW YORK.

LEFEVRE

*AMERICAN JEWELRY CO.,
CINCINNATI, OHIO.

B.B.B.

BAILEY, BANKS AND BIDDLE
Philadelphia, PA

*HENRY ALKAN,
171 Broadway,
NEW YORK.

A. ANZELEWITZ & CO.,
110 Canal St.,
NEW YORK.

*B. A. BALLOU & CO.,
61 Peck St.,
PROVIDENCE, R. I.

GOLDINE

*CHARLES H. ALLEN & CO.,
ATTLEBORO, MASS.

ATTLEBORO MFG. CO.,
ATTLEBORO, MASS.

☾ ⚓ ✕ ☆ ⬠
(Thimbles.)
BARKER MFG. CO.,
PROVIDENCE, R. I.

CENTENNIAL

*FREEMAN S. ALLEN,
WASHINGTON, D. C.
(Out of business.)

*AUSTIN & CRAW,
SOUTH NORWALK, CONN.

BARSTOW & WILLIAMS,
7 Beverly St.,
PROVIDENCE, R. I.

67

THE NEW PERFECTION
(Skirt Holder.)

(Hairpins.)
E. & J. BASS,
573 Broadway,
NEW YORK.

THE BASSETT JEWELRY CO.,
93 Sabin St.,
PROVIDENCE, R. I.

B
14 K
⚭≣

BATTIN & CO.,
Ogden St. and Third Ave.,
NEWARK, N. J.

BAUM & OPPENHEIM,
NEW YORK.
(Out of business.)

B. J. CO.
BAYLESS JEWELRY CO.,
LITTLE ROCK, ARK.

B. B. B.
BECKER & BARNETT,
481 Washington St.,
NEWARK, N. J.

B-G
BECKWITH, GRANT & CO.,
NEW YORK.
(Out of business.)

GEORGE BELL CO.,
437 17th St.,
DENVER, COL.

*BENEDICT & WARNER,
21 Maiden Lane,
NEW YORK.

B. B.
BENNETT & BRADFORD,
Succeeded by
E. A. BENNETT & CO.,
4 Blount St.,
PROVIDENCE, R. I.

*JOSEPH BENNETT & CO.,
51-53 Maiden Lane,
NEW YORK.

T. E. BENNETT CO.,
7 Beverly St.,
PROVIDENCE, R. I.

B. & B.

(On Cards.)
B. C. & B.
(Discontinued.)
BERNHEIM & BEER,
51 Maiden Lane,
NEW YORK.

CHESTER BILLINGS & SON,
58 Nassau St.,
NEW YORK.

(On gold.)   (On silver.)
JAMES BINGHAM,
719 Sansom St.,
PHILADELPHIA, PA.

B. B.
BIOREN BROS.,
473 Washington St.,
NEWARK, N. J.

BIPPART, GRISCOM & OSBORN,
32-36 Marshall St.,
NEWARK, N. J.

B.S.F.
BLACK, STARR & FROST
New York

Sterlin**E**

JAMES E. BLAKE CO.,
ATTLEBORO, MASS.

B. B.

BLISS BROS. COMPANY,
ATTLEBORO, MASS.

D. C. BOURQUIN,
PORT RICHMOND, N. Y.

(Rolled Gold Plate.)
Waarenzeichen 48 584

B RGP
Deposé — Trade Mark.
(Registered Trade-mark for Foreign Countries.)

W. J. BRAITSCH & CO.,
472 Potter's Ave.,
PROVIDENCE, R. I.

H. BRASSLER

BRIDE & TINCKLER,
336 Mulberry St.,
NEWARK, N. J.

D. F. B. CO.
CARMEN

D. F. BRIGGS CO.,
ATTLEBORO, MASS.

THOMAS F. BROGAN CO.,
26 Union Square,
NEW YORK.

D. DE W. BROKAW,
19 John St.,
NEW YORK.

M. S. B. & CO, H.
M. S. BROWN & CO.,
128-130 Granville St.,
HALIFAX, N. S.

*****PRINCESS**
(Earrings.)

J. BULOVA CO.,
51 and 53 Maiden Lane,
NEW YORK.

BURSTOW, KOLLMAR & CO.,
50 Columbia St.,
NEWARK, N. J.

(Discontinued.)
GEORGE H. CAHOONE & CO.,
7 Beverly St.,
PROVIDENCE, R. I.

J.E.C. & CO.
J.E. CALDWELL & CO.
Philadelphia, PA

EXCELSIOR

CAPRON CO.,
43 Sabin St.,
PROVIDENCE, R. I.

CARRINGTON & CO.,
1 Maiden Lane,
NEW YORK.

*CARTER, HOWE & CO.,
13 Maiden Lane,
NEW YORK.

CARTER, QVARNSTROM
& REMINGTON,
ATTLEBORO, MASS.

C 14 K.
(14 K.)
C X K
(10 K.)

(Discontinued.)

CHAMPENOIS & CO.,
50 Walnut St.,
NEWARK, N. J.

S. B. C. CO.

S. B. CHAMPLIN CO.,
116 Chestnut St.,
PROVIDENCE, R. I.

C. & B.

CHAPMAN & BARDEN,
ATTLEBORO, MASS.

JOSEPH F. CHATELLIER,
NEW YORK.
(Out of business.)

W. G. C.

W. G. CLARK & CO.,
NORTH ATTLEBORO, MASS.

FIRST CHURCH
*DAVID N. COOK,
SALEM, MASS.

*C. H. COOKE CO.,
61 Peck St.,
PROVIDENCE, R. I.

COOPER & FORMAN,
3 Maiden Lane,
NEW YORK.

D. R. CORBIN,
10 Cortlandt St.,
NEW YORK.

14 Y

W. F. CORY & BRO.,
27 Marshall St.,
NEWARK, N. J.

S. COTTLE CO.,
31 E. 17th St.,
NEW YORK.

CRANE & THEURER,
13-15 Franklin St.,
NEWARK, N. J.

CHAS. S. CROSSMAN & CO.,
3 Maiden Lane,
NEW YORK.

CUMMINGS & CO.
Attleboro, MASS.

F. H. CUTLER & CO.,
NORTH ATTLEBORO, MASS.

C & G —
(Discontinued.)
CUTLER & GRANBERY,
Succeeded by
J. A. & S. W. GRANBERY,
26 Beecher St.,
NEWARK, N. J.

*R. S. CUTTING,
PROVIDENCE, R. I.
(Out of business.)

D. & C.
THE DAGGETT & CLAP CO.,
ATTLEBORO, MASS.

OPENET
HERBERT DALGETY,
1278 Broadway,
NEW YORK.

D. 14 K.
J. D. DALZELL & CO.,
32 Marshall St.,
NEWARK, N. J.

D. F.
DATTELBAUM & FRIEDMAN,
45 John St.,
NEW YORK.

(14 K. only.)

DAY, CLARK & CO.,
21-23 Maiden Lane,
NEW YORK.

DENVER WATCH CASE CO.,
DENVER, COL.

JOS. H. DESCHAMPS,
701 Chestnut St.,
PHILADELPHIA, PA.

CHIC
*STONINE
THE APEX STUD
THE APEX VEST BUTTON
THE MAGNET

O. C. DEVEREUX & CO.,
224 Eddy St.,
PROVIDENCE, R. I.

DOLGIN & COHN,
NEW YORK.
(Out of business.)

DONLEY & CO.,
129 Eddy St.,
PROVIDENCE, R. I.

ROYAL
(Shirt Waist Holder.)
*ANNA F. DUNBAR,
ALBANY, N. Y.

DREICER & CO.

DURAND & CO.
Newark, NJ

(Hair Pins.)
W. D. EARL & CO.,
LEOMINSTER, MASS.

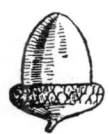

ECKFELDT & ACKLEY,
49 Chestnut St.,
NEWARK, N. J.

EHLERS & CO.,
41-43 Maiden Lane,
NEW YORK.

EISENSTADT MFG. CO.,
209-213 N. 7th St.,
ST. LOUIS, MO.

(On Cards.)
ELIASSOF BROS. & CO.,
9 Maiden Lane,
NEW YORK.

*WILLIAM M. ELIAS & BROTHER,
NEW YORK.
(Out of business.)

*
G. E. E. & CO.
GEO. E. ELLIS & CO.,
WINNIPEG, MAN.

P. W. ELLIS & CO.,
31 Wellington St., E.,
TORONTO, ONT.

MILTON L. ERNST,
30-32 Platt St.,
NEW YORK.

*ESSER & BARRY,
101 Sabin St.,
PROVIDENCE, R. I.

FISHEL, NESSLER & CO.,
556 Broadway,
NEW YORK.

FLETCHER, BURROWS & CO.,
53 Clifford St.,
PROVIDENCE, R. I.

J. FLOERSHEIM & CO.,
173-175 E. Adams St.,
CHICAGO, ILL.

*J. A. FLOMERFELT & CO.,
1 and 3 Union Sq.,
NEW YORK.

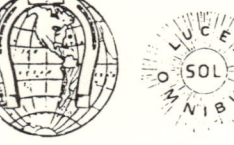

CORONA   SUNRISE
CORONADO   SUNSET
ENTERIZOS   SUPERIOR
ESTRELLA   SUPREMO
HELIOS   VICTORIA
PEERLESS   VICTORIOSO
REPORTER   20 CENTURY
SUN

R. R. FOGEL & CO.,
177 Broadway,
NEW YORK.

F

STEPHEN L. FOLGER,
180 Broadway,
NEW YORK.

FORD & CARPENTER,
101 Sabin St.,
PROVIDENCE, R. I.

*THEODORE W. FOSTER & BRO. CO.,
100 Richmond St.,
PROVIDENCE, R. I.

*FOWLER BROS.,
183 Eddy St.,
PROVIDENCE, R. I.

(Elk Jewelry.)   (Diamonds and Diamond Jewelry.)

THE GUSTAVE FOX CO.,
4 W. 4th St.,
CINCINNATI, OHIO.

CENTURY

*E. I. FRANKLIN & CO.,
NORTH ATTLEBORO, MASS.

*FRANKLIN JEWELRY CO.,
PHILADELPHIA, PA.
(Out of Business.)

FRENCH & FRANKLIN MFG. CO.,
NORTH ATTLEBORO, MASS.
(Out of business.)

HENRY FREUND & BRO.,
9 Maiden Lane,
NEW YORK.

GAULT & CO.

GEOFFROY & CO.,
170 Broadway,
NEW YORK.

GLORIEUX & CO.,
Succeeded by
SANSBURY & NELLIS,
23 Marshall St.,
NEWARK, N. J.

INGOMAR GOLDSMITH & CO.,
30 Maiden Lane,
NEW YORK.

*HARD-TO-BEAT
*PREMIER

THE GOLDSMITHS' STOCK COMPANY OF CANADA,
TORONTO, ONT.

LION, ANCHOR
G & SPREAD
EAGLE

GORHAM, INC.
Providence, RI

(10 K. Gold)

J. A. & S. W. GRANBERY,
26 Beecher St.,
NEWARK, N. J.

★ G ☾

(Discontinued.)

J. L. GRANBERY,
Succeeded by
G. P. GRANBERG,
111 E. 14th St.,
NEW YORK

G
GREENBURG & GLASER,
125 Fulton St.,
NEW YORK.

*W. C. GREENE & CO.,
101 Sabin St.,
PROVIDENCE, R. I.

CHAS. E. HANCOCK CO.,
7 Beverly St.,
PROVIDENCE, R. I.

HARVEY & OTIS,
183 Eddy St.,
PROVIDENCE, R. I.

HENRY C. HASKELL,
13 Maiden Lane,
NEW YORK.

WILLIAM W. HAYDEN CO.,
105-109 Oliver St.,
NEWARK, N. J.

73

14K H

HAYDEN MFG. CO.,
23 Maiden Lane,
NEW YORK.

A. HEINEKE

A. J. HEDGES & CO.,
14 John St.,
NEW YORK.

HERBST & WASSALL,
423 Washington Ave.,
NEWARK, N. J.

HESSELPOTH & SMETHURST,
PHILADELPHIA, PA.
(Out of business.)

*ELBERT E. HICKOK,
ST. LOUIS, MO.
(Out of business.)

H. A. CO.
H. A. & CO.

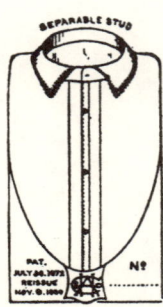

ANTI-SWEAR

HORTON, ANGELL CO.,
ATTLEBORO, MASS.

*IMPERIAL MFG. CO.,
CHICAGO, ILL.
(Out of business.)

E. B. INGRAHAM,
21 Eddy St.,
PROVIDENCE, R. I.

INTERNATIONAL JEWELRY WORK-
ERS UNION OF AMERICA,
61 St. Mark's Place,
NEW YORK.

R
(Pins and Buttons.)
20TH CENTURY CHARMS
I. & R.
(Charms.)

IRONS & RUSSELL,
102 Friendship St.,
PROVIDENCE, R. I.

J. I. S.

JEWELERS MFG. CO.,
619 16th St.,
DENVER, COL.

JOHANTGEN & KOHL,
306-308 Nicollet Ave.,
MINNEAPOLIS, MINN.

JOHNSON, HAYWARD & PIPER,
588 Broadway,
NEW YORK.

JONAS & BROD,
37 Maiden Lane,
NEW YORK.

JONES & WOODLAND,
365 Market St.,
NEWARK, N. J.

A. JORALEMON & SON,
38-40 Crawford St.,
NEWARK, N. J.

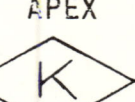

KEER & KINGSLAND,
NEWARK, N. J.
(Out of business.)

APEX

CHARLES KELLER & CO.,
11 John St.,
NEW YORK.

KELLER JEWELRY MFG. CO.,
64 Nassau St.,
NEW YORK.

KELLER MFG. CO.,
29 Gold St.,
NEW YORK.

KENT & STANLEY CO., LTD.,
PROVIDENCE, R. I.
(Out of business.)

(Bracelets.)
KENT & WOODLAND,
Successors to
WILLIAM H. BALL & CO.,
12-16 John St.,
NEW YORK.

KEYSTONE JEWELRY MFG. CO.,
ATTLEBORO, MASS.

(Discontinued.)
*WM. B. KERF
860 Broadw
NEW YORK.

(Thimbles.)
KETCHAM & McDOUGALL,
37 Maiden Lane,
NEW YORK.

KING COLLAR BUTTON CO.,
530 Broadway,
NEW YORK.

H. A. KIRBY CO.,
85 Sprague St.,
PROVIDENCE, R. I.

(Discontinued.)
KLEIN BROS.,
KLEIN BROS. CO.,
Successors
51-53 Maiden Lane.

KOEHLER, FLORENCE
Chicago, IL

KOHN AND CO.
Newark, NJ

FRANK KURSH & SON CO
23 Marshall St.
NEWARK, N. J.

LAKEWOOD CO.,
LAKEWOOD, N. J.

*SILVIUS LANDSBERG
NEW YORK.
(Out of business.)

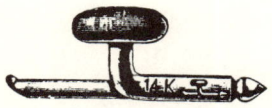

(Present Mark.)

(Old Mark.)
LARTER, ELCOX & CO.,
21-23 Maiden Lane,
NEW YORK.

CORRECT EVENING DRESS
PEER
QUARTZINE
THE REQUISITE
TWINKLER

LAWTON & CO.,
PAWTUCKET, R. I.

LAWTON, SPENCER & SHERMAN,
PROVIDENCE, R. I.
(Out of business.)

ROYAL

ROYAL 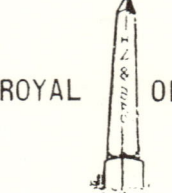 OBELISK

HENRY FOERSTE & BRO.,
Eddy St.
PROVIDENCE, R. I.

ACME
COLUMBIA
EIFFEL
EMPIRE
EUREKA
HERCULES
KNICKERBOCKER
NEWPORT
NONPAREIL
SENSIBLE
THE TWINS
UNEEDA
UNIVERSAL
UTOPIA
VICTOR
YANKEE

S. & B. LEDERER CO.,
100 Stewart St.,
PROVIDENCE, R. I.

GEO. H. LEES & CO.,
17 Main St. E.,
HAMILTON, ONT., CANADA.

E. A. LEHMANN & CO.,
20 Maiden Lane,
NEW YORK.

HENRY L. LEIBE MFG. CO.,
Succeeded by
C. F. KEES & CO.,
24 Boudinot St.,
NEWARK, N. J.

CHARLES M. LEVY,
90 William St.,
NEW YORK.

F. L. & CO.
FERD. LEVY & CO.,
929 Chestnut St.,
PHILADELPHIA, PA.

LEWIS BROS.,
38 Maiden Lane,
NEW YORK.

(Discontinued.)
*LEWIS, KAISER & LUTHY,
Succeeded by
DAVID KAISER & CO.,
12 John St.,
NEW YORK.

LEYS, CHRISTIE & CO.,
65 Nassau St.,
NEW YORK.

WILLIAM LINK,
NEWARK, N. J.

LINK & ANGELL,
13 Franklin St.,
NEWARK, N. J.

LINK, ANGELL & WEISS,
Succeeded by
LINK & ANGELL,
13 Franklin St.,
NEWARK, N. J.

D. LISNER & CO.,
140 Fifth Ave., corner 19th St.,
NEW YORK.

*LISSAUER & CO.,
12 Maiden Lane,
NEW YORK.

W. L. & CO.
*WM. LOEB & CO.,
101 Sabin St.,
PROVIDENCE, R. I.

GILT EDGE
*H. C. LUTHER & CO.,
PROVIDENCE, R. I.
(Out of business.)

WM. H. LUTHER & SON,
214 Oxford St.,
PROVIDENCE, R. I.

14K
(10 K. Goods.)
MANDEVILLE, CARROW & CRANE,
332 Mulberry St.,
NEWARK, N. J.

(On Cards.)
M. MANNIST & CO.,
NEW YORK.
(Out of Business.)

WALDORF-ASTORIA
MARDEN & KETTLETY,
7 Beverly St.,
PROVIDENCE, R. I.

M. & P.
MARSELLUS & PITT,
2 Maiden Lane,
NEW YORK.

 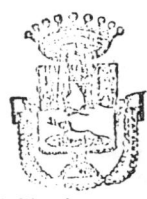
(Rolled Plate.)

(Electro Plate.)
MASON, HOWARD & CO.,
ATTLEBORO, MASS.

J. T. MAURAN MFG. CO.,
61 Peck St.,
PROVIDENCE, R. I.

JOS. MAYER & BROS.,
116 Cherry St.,
SEATTLE, WASH.

*E. S. McLAUGHLIN & CO.,
157 Orange St.,
PROVIDENCE, R. I.

WELLWORTH

*McRAE & KEELER,
ATTLEBORO, MASS.

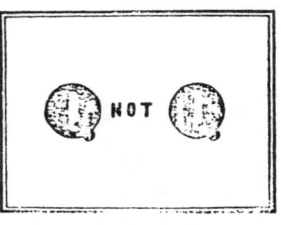
JOS. H. MEYER & BROS.,
909 Broadway,
BROOKLYN, N. Y.

RUBBER NECK
(Badges.)
*MILWAUKEE NOVELTY CO.,
MILWAUKEE, WIS.

*MOSBACHER & CO.,
105 Water St.,
NEW YORK.

(Discontinued.)
*H. MUHR'S SONS,
1110 Chestnut St.,
PHILADELPHIA, PA.

(Jewelry and Silverware.)

S. F. MYERS CO.,
48 Maiden Lane,
NEW YORK.

BRUCE MURPHY,
ORILLIA, ONT., CAN.

*****EUGENE NAEGELE,**
PHILADELPHIA, PA.
(Out of business.)

NESLER & CO.,
38 Crawford St.,
NEWARK, N. J.

(Discontinued.)

ODENHEIMER, ZIMMERN & CO.,
Succeeded by
ZIMMERN, REES & CO.,
13 Maiden Lane,
NEW YORK.

O 18 D

OLIVER & DAVIS,
3a Maiden Lane,
NEW YORK.

R. OLIVER & BLOOMFIELD   **O 18 B**

RICHARD OLIVER & BLOOMFIELD,
Succeeded by
OLIVER & DAVIS,
3a Maiden Lane,
NEW YORK.

XIX CENTURY HEIRLOOM

*****FRANK N. OSBORNE,**
NEW YORK.

OSMUN-PARKER MFG. CO.,
338 Mulberry St.,
NEWARK, N. J.

*****WILLIAM L. PAINE,**
ARGENTA, ARK.
(Out of business.)

PEACOCK & CO.
Chicago, IL

HENRY PEARCE,
1667 Notre Dame St.,
MONTREAL, QUE.

PIPE-STEM

Big Bonanza

THE WORLD LEVER

*****PARKS BROS. & ROGERS,**
7 Beverly St.,
PROVIDENCE, R. I.

*****D. C. PERCIVAL & CO.,**
373 Washington St.,
BOSTON, MASS.

18 P.   **15 P.**   **14 P.**

PERLEY BROS.,
26 John St.,
NEW YORK.

EL PERFECTO
*FRANCIS PERNAS,
130 Pearl St.,
NEW YORK.

H. B. P. & CO.
H. B. PETERS & CO.,
177 Broadway,
NEW YORK.

BRUMMEL
*PFAELZER BROS. & CO.,
Succeeded by
RITTER, KAHN & CO.,
1315 Market St.,
PHILADELPHIA, PA.

 PROPOSAL
BONE
ALBERT PFEIFER,
LITTLE ROCK, ARK.,
and 9-11 Maiden Lane,
NEW YORK.

*PHILADELPHIA OPTICAL & WATCH CO.,
PHILADELPHIA, PA.
(Out of business.)

PHOENIX JEWELRY CO.,
41-43 Maiden Lane,
NEW YORK.

*PLAINVILLE STOCK CO.,
PLAINVILLE, MASS.

(Discontinued.)
E. A. POTTER & CO.,
71 Peck St.,
PROVIDENCE, R. I.

POWERS & MAYER,
260 Fifth Ave.,
NEW YORK.

THOMAS QUAYLE & CO.,
100 Richmond St.,
PROVIDENCE, R. I.

*DIAMONETTE

REGNELL, BIGNEY & CO.,
ATTLEBORO, MASS.

R. M. CO.
RENOMMEE MFG. CO.,
NEWARK, N. J.

HYGEA
REX KING

THE REXFORD CO.,
1024 Market St.,
PHILADELPHIA, PA.

RHODES BROS. & ROTHSCHILD,
ATTLEBORO, MASS.

*BENEDICT
ENOS RICHARDSON & CO.,
21-23 Maiden Lane,
NEW YORK.

RIKER BROS.,
42-44 Hill St.,
NEWARK, N. J.

R. & F.
RILEY, FRENCH & HEFFRON,
NORTH ATTLEBORO, MASS.

(Quality stamped in center, either 22 K., 20 K., 18 K., or 14 K.)
*RIPLEY-HOWLAND MFG. CO.,
21 Bromfield St.,
BOSTON, MASS.

CMR

R&B
(Discontinued.)
CHAS. M. ROBBINS CO.,
ATTLEBORO, MASS.

79

ROBINSON & CO.,
SOUTH ATTLEBORO, MASS.

R. & S.
ROEHM & SON,
184-186 Woodward Ave.,
DETROIT, MICH.

ROGERS, S.L. & GEORGE & CO.
Hartford, CONN.

A. ROSENBERG,
50 Columbia St.,
NEWARK, N. J.

DEFENDER
FREE CUBA
GOOD LUCK
GOOD LUCK, MANILA
MANILA
MICARDO
MIKADO
ROSE LEAF
THE FAV.
THE FAVORITE
THE FEDERATION
THE LEADER
THE LEADING NOVELTY
THE STATES
GEO. H. ROSENBLATT,
229 Broadway,
NEW YORK.

ROSENTHAL MFG. CO.,
3152 Cottage Grove Ave.,
CHICAGO, ILL.

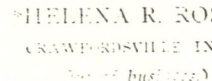
HELENA R. ROST,
CRAWFORDSVILLE, IND.
(Out of business.)

*CARL L. ROST,
CRAWFORDSVILLE, IND.
(Out of business.)

ROTHSCHILD BROS. CO.,
ATTLEBORO, MASS.

L. J. ROY & CO.,
53 Clifford St.,
PROVIDENCE, R. I.

ROY & MINAHAN,
PROVIDENCE, R. I.
(Out of business.)

L. W. R.

L. W. RUBENSTEIN,
54 Maiden Lane,
NEW YORK.

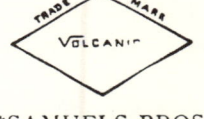
*SAMUELS BROS.,
YOUNGSTOWN, O.

H. & A. SAUNDERS,
King and Bay Sts.,
TORONTO, ONT.

(14 K. and 18 K.)
NIC. SCHELNIN CO.,
108 W. 18th St.,
NEW YORK.

(On Stationery and Jewelry Cards.)

(Discontinued.)
SCHRADER-WITTSTEIN CO.,
103 State St.,
CHICAGO, ILL.

SHREVE & CO.
San Francisco, CA

THE BRILLIANTINA
J. SCHWARZKOPF & CO.,
7 Beverly St.,
PROVIDENCE, R. I.

(Discontinued.)
SCOFIELD & DE WYNGAERT,
48 Walnut St.,
NEWARK, N. J.

S. M. & S.
(On Cards Only.)
SCOFIELD, MELCHER & SCOFIELD,
PLAINVILLE, MASS.

(Gold Jewelry.)
WM. L. SEXTON & CO.,
7 Maiden Lane,
NEW YORK.

ERNEST R. SHIPTON,
LONDON, ENGLAND.

PAYE & BAKER MFG. CO.,
NORTH ATTLEBORO, MASS.

SIMONS, BRO. & CO.,
611 Sansom St.,
PHILADELPHIA, PA.

SLOAN & CO.,
21-23 Maiden Lane,
NEW YORK.

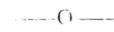
(10K. Letters.)   (14K. Letters.)
C. SYDNEY SMITH & CO.,
13 Maiden Lane,
NEW YORK.

GEO. J. SMITH & CO.,
13 Maiden Lane,
NEW YORK.

T. I. SMITH & CO.,
NORTH ATTLEBORO, MASS.

SMITH & CROSBY,
ATTLEBORO, MASS.

SNOW & WESTCOTT,
21 Maiden Lane,
NEW YORK.

ADAMANTINA
J. SOLINGER & CO.,
9 Calender St.,
PROVIDENCE, R. I.

J. J. S.
(On Goods.)
J. J. S. & CO.
(On Cards and Tissues.)
J. J. SOMMER & CO.,
NORTH ATTLEBORO, MASS.

S. M. CO.
S. & M.
SOMMER & MILLS CO.,
Succeeded by
J. J. SOMMER & CO.,
NORTH ATTLEBORO, MASS.

SPIER & FORSHEIM,
37-39 Maiden Lane,
NEW YORK.

*STEINAU JEWELRY CO.,
CINCINNATI, O.
(Out of business.)

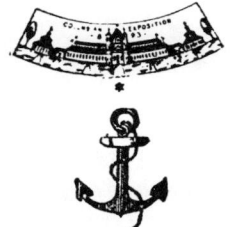
(Thimbles.)
STERN BROS. & CO.,
43 Gold St.,
NEW YORK.

L. M. & CO., LTD.
*CHAS. H. STONE,
117 W. 58th St.,
NEW YORK.

GEO. O. STREET & SONS,
24 John St.,
NEW YORK.

GEO. O. STREET & SONS,
15 John St.,
NEW YORK.

STREETER BROTHERS,
ATTLEBORO, MASS.

THE DEFENDER
FAIR HARVARD
LITTLE BILLIE
HERE'S A GOOD OLD YALE
PRINCETON

J. F. STURDY'S SONS,
ATTLEBORO FALLS, MASS.

LEUSAIC
*THAYER MANUFACTURING JEWELRY CO.,
ASTORIA, N. Y.

PHILIPP THOMA,
21 John St.,
NEW YORK.

TIFFANY & CO.,
Union Sq. and 15th St.,
NEW YORK.

*TILLINGHAST & ALBRO,
PROVIDENCE, R. I.
(Out of business.)

(14 K. Gold Only.)
CHAS. L. TROUT & CO.,
15 Maiden Lane,
NEW YORK.

UDALL & BALAU

*UNITED SOCIETY OF CHRISTIAN ENDEAVOR,
BOSTON, MASS.

GEO. L. VOSE & CO.,
59 Clifford St.,
PROVIDENCE, R. I.

*WAITE, MATHEWSON & CO.,
140 Orange St.,
PROVIDENCE, R. I.

(Discontinued.)
*A. WALLACH & CO.,
39 Maiden Lane,
NEW YORK.

WALTON & CO.

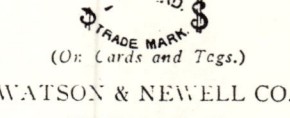

(On Cards and Tags.)
WATSON & NEWELL CO.,
ATTLEBORO, MASS.

F. A. WATTENBERG & CO.,
12 John St.,
NEW YORK.

G. K. WEBSTER,
NORTH ATTLEBORO, MASS.

*WEINMANN & CO.,
1215 Arch St.,
PHILADELPHIA, PA.

GEO. WETTSTEIN,
CEDAR RAPIDS, IA.

H. WEXEL & CO.,
ATTLEBORO, MASS.
(Out of Business.)

WEYHING BROS. & CO.,
16 John R. St.,
DETROIT, MICH.

J. J. WHITE & CO.,
26 Fountain St.,
PROVIDENCE, R. I.

(On 14 K.)
WHITESIDE & BLANK,
Liberty and Lafayette Sts.,
NEWARK, N. J.

W. & D.
ALICE NIELSEN
FLORODORA
YO SAN

WHITING & DAVIS,
PLAINVILLE, MASS.

F. G. WHITNEY & CO.,
ATTLEBORO, MASS.
(Out of business.)

WIGHTMAN & HOUGH CO.,
7 Beverly St.,
PROVIDENCE, R. I.

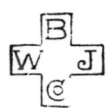

A. J. WILD JEWELRY CO.,
104 N. 6th St.,
ST. LOUIS, MO.

SIMPLICITÉ

F. D. WILLIAMS,
PROVIDENCE, R. I.
(Out of Business.)

CHESTERFIELD
(On Link-Button Cards.)
WILLIAMS & PAYTON,
59 Page St.,
PROVIDENCE, R. I.

W. H. WILMARTH & CO.,
ATTLEBORO, MASS.

P. E. WITHERELL,
ATTLEBORO, MASS.

(Rolled Gold.)
L. WIESENHAUSEN,
37 Maiden Lane,
NEW YORK.

Some American Jewelers without Registered Marks

Name	Location	Identifying Initials or Mark
Bailey, Banks & Biddle	Philadelphia	B.B.B. or B.B.& B.
H. Birks	Canada	Lion and B.B.
Black, Starr & Frost	New York	B.S.F.
H. Brassler*	——	——
J. E. Caldwell & Co.	Philadelphia	J.E.C.
Cummings & Co.	Attleboro, Mass.	—
Dreicer & Co.	New York	——
Durand & Co.	Newark, N.J.	——
Gault & Co.	——	——
Gorham, Inc.	Providence	Lion, anchor, G, spread eagle
A. Heineke*	——	——
Kalo*	Chicago	——
A. Knight	——	——
Florence Koehler*	Chicago	——
Kohn & Co.	Newark, N.J.	——
Lebolt	Chicago	——
Peacock & Co.	Chicago	——
Potter-Mellen*	Chicago	——
S. L. & George Rogers & Co.	Hartford, Conn.	Acorn
Shreve & Co.	San Francisco	——
Spaulding & Co.	Chicago	——
D. S. Spaulding	Mansfield, Mass.	——
T.B. Starr	New York	——
Udall & Balau	New York	——
Walton & Co.	——	——
R. Yard & Co.	New York	——
F. Zernkilton	Philadelphia	——

*Arts and Crafts style jewelry.

French Jewelers and Goldsmiths Circa 1900.
PARIS JEWELERS WITH REGISTERED MARKS

Owl in oval imported pieces—chiefly gold from 1892.

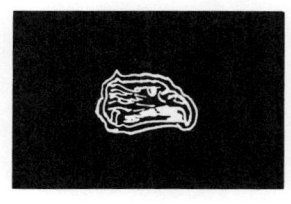

Eagle's Head, made in France 1847 to 1919.

An imported foreign gold that met French standard 1864 to 1893.

Made of platinum.

Name	Description of Mark	Initials or Words Appearing on Mark
ACHARD (L)	Antique chariot	L.A.
ALAMARGOT (A)	Note on a musical bar	A.A.
ALBARET (EUG)	Ring pierced by an arrow	E.A.
ALBESSARD (C)	Bagpipe	C.A.
ALEXANDRE (G)	Horse's head	G.A.
ALLAIX (L)	Cross of Lorraine	L.A.
AMIEL (J)	Two-pointed hat	J.A.
ANCELOT (E)	Horseshoe nail	E.A.
ANQUETIN (M)	*All or nothing*	M.A.
ANSART (D)	Tongs	D.A.
ARFVIDSON (C)	Dove pierced by an arrow	C.A.
ARON (F)	Ace of hearts with star	——
ARNOULD, A.	Thistle	A.A.
ARPIN (FERD)	Pine	F.A.
ARTHAUD (V)	Artichoke	V.A.
ASTORGUE (CLAUDE)	Turtle	C.A.
AUBERT (FREDERIC)	Coat of mail	F.A.
AUBERY (CH)	*C.A.* surmounted by star	C.A.
AUCOC (A)	Spearhead surmounted by cock	A.A.
AUCOC FILS (L)	Wolf passing left	L.A.
AUFORT (F)	Porter carrying sack on shoulder	F.A.

Name	Description of Mark	Initials or Words Appearing on Mark
AUGER (ALPHONSE)	Star in a square	A.A.
AUVRAY (L)	Two hands crosswise in upper part, separated by grenade	L.A.
AUXOEUFS (H)	Eggs	H.A.
AUZOLLE (L)	Hooded cape	L.A.
AZEMA (P)	Hunting horn, star in center	P.A.
BABARIT (H)	An eagle holding a spoon and fork in his claw	H.B.
BAC (GUILLAUME)	Pencil case and pen folder in form of cross	G.B.
BACHELARD ET PERIN	Boat	B.P.
BAGET (GEORGES)	Stocking	G.B.
BAILHACHE (ERNEST)	Axe	E.B.
BALLIN (ALEXIS)	Make-up case	A.P.
BAMBERGER (S)	Bamboo cane	S.B.
BANCON (A)	Clover leaf in a crescent	B. FRERES
BANSEE (EUG)	Standing lion	E.B.
BAPST (J ET P)	East	C.B.
BARBARE (THEOPHILE)	Rule	T.B.
BARBEDIENNE (F)	Shield of Paris in the middle, five stars above	F.B.
BAROUX (C)	Bar on adverb "where"	C.B.
BARRAL (EUG)	Barrel	E.B.
BARRO (T)	Seven-pointed star	T.B.
BATAILLE (JEAN)	Helmet	J.B.
BAUDET (L)	Donkey	BAUDET
BAUER (JACOB)	Butterfly	J.B.
BAUVE (H)	Carriage step	H.B.
BEAUCHARD (EMILE)	Chariot	E.B.
BEAUDOIN (ANTONY)	Shield	A.B.
BEAUJEUX (CONS)	Daisy	C.B.
BECHE (EMILE)	Spade and paddle in form of cross	E.B.
BECHE (J)	Spade	J.B.
BECK (MAURICE)	Four-leaf clover	M.B.
BEGARD (ERNEST)	Natural (music sign)	E. Begard
BEGARD (HORTENSE)	Two stars	H.B.
BEGAT (ANGRE)	Carpenter's plane	A.B.
BELIN (RENE)	Cornet	R.B.
BENNEZON (JULES)	Fish hook	J.B.
BENOIST (E)	Dragonfly	E.B.

Name	Description of Mark	Initials or Words Appearing on Mark
BENOIST (LOUIS)	Pansy	L.B.
BENOIT (EMILE)	Ant	E.B.
BENSE (EDGAR)	Clover leaf	E.B.
BERARD (G)	Pineapple	G.B.
BERARDO (STEP)	Fish	S.B.
BERGER ET NEUMAN	Chair	B.N.
BERGER (SALOMON)	Pendulum	S.B.
BERGES (FR)	Ram	F.B.
BERLIN (HENRI)	Ring of watch	H.B.
BERNARD (M)	Star below	M.B.
BERNARDIN (AD)	Bore saw	A.B.
BERTHET (H)	Bunch of grapes	H.B.
BERTRAND	Monkey	B. et F.
BERTRAND (EMILE)	Crozier	E.B.
BESCHER	Spade of the wise men	B.A.
BESEGHER (GASTON)	Die with goblet beneath three hearts in triangle	G.B.
BESSAN ET WISSAERT	Oval hair curler	B. et W.
BESSON (A)	Open hand	A.B.
BESSON (E)	Two cupids embracing	E.B.
BETOUILLE (AUGUSTE)	A square formed by four beads	A.B.
BEUNKE (RODOLPHE)	Winnowing basket	R.B.
BIAIS ET NOIROT-BIAIS	Two key crosses	B.A.
BIARD (LUCHIEN)	Tongs	L.B.
BIADAULT (HENRI)	Daisy	H.B.
BIELI (EUG)	Dolphin	E.B.
BIGNON, AMMER ET C	Several buttons	B.A. et C.
BILLAULT (LEON)	Key	L.B.
BING (SIEGFRIED)	An *A* on an *N*	S.B.
BOIN ET FREMINET	Hydrangea	B. et F.
BIZOLIER, NIDRICHE ET C.	Coffee pot	B. et N.
BLACHE (RENE)	Axe	R.B.
BLANADET (E)	Ewer	E.B.
BLANCHET (GUSTAVE)	Purse	G.B.
BLANVILLAIN (HANRI)	Stopper	H.B.
BLART (ALFRED)	Ram's head, star below	A.B.
BLAVAT ET ARNOUD	Peaked cap	H.B.
BLED (G)	Black wheat or buckwheat	G.B.
BLUM (ALBERT)	A bird feather silver cased	A.B.
BLUM (MAURICE)	Wild rose	M.B.

Name	Description of Mark	Initials or Words Appearing on Mark
BLUM (SYLVAIN)	Violet	S.B.
BOIN (GEORGES)	Stool	BOIN
BOIRE (ADRIEN)	Mortar firing a rocket	A.B.
BOIRIER (A)	Cardinal's hat	A.B.
BOIVIN (V)	Two stars and crescent inverted	V.B.
BON (JULES)	Daisy with star center	J.B.
BONALGUES (CH)	Bent bow and arrow	C.B.
BONANGE-DUVAL	Head of angel	D.B.
BONNESOEUR (EDM)	Lyre between two beads	E.B.
BONNET (E)	Bishop's mitre	E.B.
BORELLE (PIERRE)	Piece of chain	P.B.
BOUCHER (JULES)	Butcher's gun	J.B.
BOUCHER (PAUL)	Knife	P.B.
BOUCHERON (F)	Stopper with wax from bottle of bee	F.B.
BOUCHEVEREAU (M)	A man's mouth	M.B.
BOUCHON (FELIX)	Champagne bottle with stopper	F.B.
BOUDET (VICTOR)	Lion standing	V.B.
BOUDEVILLE (ALPH)	Double ladder	A.B.
BOUDIN (EMILE)	Spiral spring	E.B.
BOULARD (LUCIEN)	Chocolate bar	L.B.
BOULARD (LEON)	Bolt	L.B.
BOULENGER (CH) ET CIE	Crescent surrounded by stars	A.B.
BOURDAIS (MARCEL)	Caduceus	M.B.
BOURDIER (T)	Bell clapper with arrow	T.B.
BOURDIN (C)	Desk	C.B.
BOURGEOIS (LEON)	Plain cake	L.B.
BOURGEOIS (NICOLAS)	Lighted lamp	N.B.
BOURGEOIS (NICOLAS)	Windmill	N.B.
BOURGEOIS (VVE)	Shield	V.B.
BOURGET (VALLERY)	Bud from vine	V.B.
BOURQUARDEZ (ALPH)	Pear between two leaves	A.B.
BOURSOT (FERD)	Bucket	F.B.
BOUSCATIE ET FROMENTI	Signet ring with a brillant	F.B.
BOUTET (RAOUL)	Sun	R.B.
BOUTILLIER (A)	Bottle	A.B.
BOUTON (P)	Rose stem with three buds	P.B. et C.
BOUTROUILLE (PAUL)	Crescent with a chalice and a shining host above it	P.B.

Name	Description of Mark	Initials or Words Appearing on Mark
BOUVIER (F)	Ox head	F.B.
BOUVIER (JULES)	Oak leaf	J.B.
BOYER (ALB)	Dog's head with open jaws	A.B.
BOYER (ALEXANDRE)	Barking dog	A.B.
BOYER-CALLOT	Chalice surmounted by crown of count	BOYER-CALLOT
BRAILLY-DEMARQUAY	Star and crescent	B.D.
BRANDEBOURG (FRANCOIS)	Passementerie	F.B.
BRANDIN (ARSENE)	Star with three beads in center	A.B.
BRASSART (CHARLES)	Arm band of first communion	C.B.
BRASSEUR (ALEX)	Tankard	A.B.
BREANT ET COULBAUX	Hammer	A.B.
BREDILLARD (ALEXANDRE)	Oval watch with star below	A.B.
BREMONT (EUG)	Pansy	E.B.
BRETEAU (HIPPOLYTE)	Boat with lateen sail	H.B.
BREVAL (CH)	Clover	C.B.
BRICTEUX (ANTOINE)	Brig	A.B.
BROCARD	Ladder	B. Freres
BROCHONT (LEON)	Flexible ring	L.B.
BROCHU (LOUIS)	Pike	L.B.
BRUGEL (M)	Heart	M.B.
BRUNET (PAUL)	Mitre	P.B.
BUCHILLOT ET CIE	Compass with a heart between the ends	B. et C.
BUFFAT (ALPH)	Chest	A.B.
BUNET (VICTOR)	Pheasant	V.B.
BAQUET (PAUL)	Wing of Mercury with star above	P.B.
BURET (LOUIS)	Cruet	L.B.
BUSSON (D)	Cat's paw between two stars	D.B.
BUTELOT (L)	Knoll surrounded with water	L.B.
CABARET (AUG)	Cross	CABARET
CADET-MILLET (EDMOND)	Pony	E.C.
CAEN (E)	Two open hands	E.C.
CAILAR ET BAYARD	Sun	C. et B.
CAILLAT (A)	Two anchors	A.C.
CAILLEMER (AUG)	Trowel	A.C.
CAILLOUX (M)	Quail perched on staff	M.C.
CALPINI (LOUIS)	Notebook	L.C.

Name	Description of Mark	Initials or Words Appearing on Mark
CANAPLE (EMILE)	Baby carriage	E.C.
CANAUX (PAUL)	Anvil	P.C. et C.
CAPRON (ANTOINE)	Cruet	A.C.
CAPY (OMER)	Cap	O.C.
CARBONNIER (LOUIS)	Vase	L.C.
CAREANAGUES (A)	Pomegranate with two leaves	A.C.
CARDEILHAC	Cross of honor and crescent	E.C.
CARDOT (L)	Mug of water	L.C.
CARETTE (ARMAND)	A above and star below name	CARETTE
CARILLON (DENIS)	Bell	D.C.
CARPENTIER (GEORGES)	Bee	G.C.
CARTAUX (FRANCOIS)	Small cask	F.C.
CARTIER (L)	Ace of hearts	L.C.
CASAULTA (J)	Lathe	J.C.
CASTEILLO (LOUIS)	Small tower	L.C.
CAUVAIN (JULES)	Cup	J.C.
CAUVAIN (L)	A square	L.C.
CAUVIN ET CIE	Thistle between two leaves	E.C.
CAVASIER (ADOLPHE)	Faucet	A.C.
CAZEZYEN (ONNIK)	Arrow in circle	O.C.
CHAILLOUS (ALEX)	Cat playing with ball	A.C.
CHAIN ET PEQUIGNOT	Count's crown	C.P.
CHAMPION	Mushroom	M.C.
CHAMPION (OCTAVE)	Cross, a crescent inverted, a bead	O.C.
CHAMPLON (ERNEST)	Horseshoe	E.C.
CHANTRE (ANGE)	Angel	A.C.
CHANTRIER (LOUIS)	Ace of clubs	L.C.
CHAPUS (ALBERT)	Sheaf	A.C.
CHARBONNET (CH)	Antique chariot	C.C.
CHARLUEX (L)	Lock of hair	L.C.
CHARPENTIER (E)	Square	E.C.
CHARPENTIER (T)	Sea wolf	T.C.
CHATELAIN (PH)	Drawing crayon	P.C.
CHAUMET (JOSEPH)	Crescent star	J.C.
CHAVETON (R)	String bean	R.C.
CHEMELAT (CH)	Open razor surmounted by crown	C.C.
CHERFILS (GEORGES)	Blunderbuss in a triangle	G.C. et Cie

Name	Description of Mark	Initials or Words Appearing on Mark
CHESNY (LEOPOLD)	Wind rose	L.C.
CHEVALET ET IORDA	Easel	C.I.
CHEVALIER (B)	Helmet	B.C.
CHEVREAU (EDOUARD)	Fawn	E.C.
CHIQUET (CAMILLE)	Coil of hair	C.C.
CHOIDECKER ET DESPREZ	Square	C.D.
CHOISNET (GEORGES)	Hedgehog	G.C.
CHOUVILLE (JULES)	Nail	J.C.
CHRETUEB (LOUIS)	Head of baby	L.C.
CHRISTOFLE ET CIE	A bee between two C's, three stars above scale with two C's	C.C.
CHRISTOTLE ET CIE	A bee below, four stars above	C.C.
CLAIRE (AUG)	A bugle and two stars	A.C.
CLASENS-LUNARDI	An anchor surmounted by eight-pointed star	C.L.
CLAUDE (ALPHONSE)	Tiger's head between initials	A.C.
CLEMENT (CAMILLE)	Key	C.C.
CLERAY (EUGENE)	Door key and line beneath	E.C.
COELLE (M. ELISABETH)	Four crescents back to back	E.C. et Cie
COIGNET (L)	Carvery set crosswise	L.C.
COL (ANTOININ)	Collar	A.C.
COL (CHARLES)	Pair of cuff links	C.Col
COLIN (EMILE)	Two leaves	C.E. et Cie
COLLEAU (A)	Collar with tie	A.C.
COLLEAU (ALB)	Pineapple	A.C.
COLLET (GEORGES)	Salt scoop	G.C.
COLOMBO (CELESTIN)	Dove	C.C.
COMPERE (V)	Rabbit	V.E.C.
CORNIOT (PIERRE)	Hunting horn	P.C.
COTARD (JULES)	Bell card	J.C.
COULON (B)	Napkin ring	B.C.
COULON	Brass pencil	D.C.
CREUZAT (LOUIS)	Crucible	L.C.
CROSNIER (BENNUS)	Handlebar of bicycle	B.C.
CROSSARD (CHARLES)	Bishop's croizier	C.C.
CURT (L)	Racket	L.C.
CUZEAUX (GEORGES)	A well surmounted by a star	G.C.

Name	Description of Mark	Initials or Words Appearing on Mark
DASSONVALLE	Dial	A.D.
DAUVERGNE (JULES)	Sword	J.D.
DAVID (CH)	Fox	C.D.
DEBAIN (ALPHOUSE)	Woodcock	A.D.
DE BOT (BIJ)	Boot	D.B.
DEBUT (ANTOINE)	Two goals	A.D.
DECHALOTTE (EMILE)	Cat standing, star above	E.D.
DECOMBIS (ATHANASE)	Head of fox	A.D.
DEFRIZE (JULES)	Open pliers	J.D.
DEGORCE (F)	Fern	F.D.
DEGOUY (CH)	Gear wheel	C.D.
DEJOUY (JULES)	Street stall	J.D.
DELAHAIS (JULES)	Sewing needle, star above	J.D.
DELAIRE (EMILE)	Crowned falcon	E.D.
DELAMARE (E)	Musical note La	E.D.
DELARBRE (CHARLES)	A tree, *DE* below	C.D.
DELARUE (F)	Woman's bust	F.D.
DELASSELLE (ALEXANDRE)	Saddle	A.D.
DELATTRE (EUGENE)	Shepherd's basket	E.D.
DELATRE (JUSTIN)	Ostrich feather, two stars on top	J.D.
DELION	Lion's claw	J.D.
DELOBELLE (LOUIS)	Ball clock	L.D.
DELORD (SYLVAIN)	Daisy	S.D.
DEMARE (VICTOR)	Eyeglasses	V.D.
DEMESMAECKER (G)	Cat's head with *M* in the middle	G.D.
DERIOT (E)	Phoenix	E. Dériot
DESAIDE (ALPH)	Head of griffin	A.D.
DESBAZEILLE (G)	Star in a lozenge	G.D.
DESCARTES (EMILE)	Two fan-shaped cards below *E.D.*	E.D.
DESFRICHES (HENRI)	Head of parrot	H.D.
DESGODETS ET GERARD	A bowl with brush inside	D.G.
DESMONS (BERNARD)	Devil's head with horns	B.D.
DESOYE (ERNEST)	Bee	E.D.
DESPRES (FELIX)	A sphere, word *gold* above and number *18* below	F.D.
DESSIMOND ET C	A 10 centine coin with hill above	D et CIE

Name	Description of Mark	Initials or Words Appearing on Mark
DETOT	Scale	E.D.
DEUTSCH (V)	A heart and crescent in center	L.D.
DIETS (FERNAUD)	A sharp in letter *D*	F.D.
DORDIS (ALFRED)	Scythe	A.D.
DORTET (AMRIUS)	A small baker's brush	M.D.
DORVILLE (A)	Wheelbarrow	A.D.
DOUILLARD (CLAUDIUS)	French horn	C.D.
DOUTRELONG (GEORGES)	Etcher's needle	G.D.
DREUX (CELESTINE)	Open umbrella	C.D.
DREUX (PAUL)	Forget-me-not	P.D.
DROT (FERDINAND)	Head of partridge, star above	F.D
DUBOIS FRERES	Hat	DEBOIS FRERES
DUCLOS ET GOUFFE	Sunset	D. et G.
DUGUINE CEMENT	Dog's head	C.D.
DUHAZE (E)	Two antique swords crosswise	E.D.
DUJARRIE ET NICOT	Tobacco leaf	D.N.
DUMAS (CH)	A back comb	C.D.
DUMAY (EUGENE)	Tongs	E.D.
DUMONT	Two hands entertwined	G.D. et C.
DUPARC LENFANT ET C	A die, a bird's wing	D.L.
DUPONT FILE (EUGENE)	Bolt and nut	T.D.
DUPONT FRERES	Three bead triangle	D.F.
DUPONT	Arch of bridge	F.D.
DUPRESSOIR (EMILE)	Printing press	E.D.
DURAND (E)	Earring	E.D.
DURBEE (EDOUARD)	A die to emboss	E.D.
DURIF (AUG)	Black bird	A.D.
DUSEAUX (VVE)	A Greek cross with a dove above	Vve. D.
DUSOUCHET	Etruscan vase	L.D.
DUTARTRE	Two hands intertwined	F.D.
DUTEIL (FRANCOIS)	An eye	F.D.
DUTHEIL (JULES)	Oak leaf	J.D.
DUVAL (CHARLES)	Star on top of a sphere	C.D.
DUVAL (JULIEN)	Bough of mistletoe	J.D.
ECK (ERN)	Two stars placed vertically, separated by a bead	E.E.

Name	Description of Mark	Initials or Words Appearing on Mark
EDAN ET RODHAIN	Two stars	E.R.
ENAULT (ROBERT)	Football	R.E.
ERNIE (EDOUARD)	Garter	E.E.
ESCROIGNARD-COLLET	Shirt button	E.C.
ESPINASSE (GUSTAVE)	Ace of clubs	G.E.
FACHATTE (BIJ)	Two hearts entwined	T.F.
FALCONNET (LOUIS)	Serpent in the form of an 8	L.F.
FALCONNET (PAUL)	Ace of clubs	P.F.
FALGUIERES (GABRIEL)	Cross of Lorraine	G.F.
FALKENBERG (GEORGES)	A falcon	G.F.
FALIZE (LUCIEN)	A ring and a pearl	L.F.
FANNIERE FRERES	Two hands entwined with falcon head	FANNIERE F.
FARDOUE (ALFRED)	Lighthouse	A.F.
FAURE (C)	Sickle	C.F.
FAVIER (L)	Entire name with a cruet above and four beads below	FAVIER
FAVRE	A clover and a star	N.F.
FAYOLLE (X)	A yawl	X.F.
FEAU (ALF)	Buffalo	A.F.
FECHOZ (GEORGES)	Rosebush	G.F.
FEJARD (E)	Head of swan	E.F.
FERON (PAUL)	Horseshoe	P.F
FETU (EMILE)	A duck	E.F.
FEUILLATRE (EUGENE)	Leaf of rosebush	E.F.
FILLIEUX (ARGENTEUR)	Two seals curved	E.F.
FIOT (CELESTIN)	A ladder above	C. Fiot
FLAMME (EDMOND)	A flame	E.F.
FLEURET (FRANCOIS)	Fencing foil	F.F.
FLINOIS (AUGUSTE)	A bicycle	A.F.
FLOCON (ERNEST)	Falcon, star above head	E.F.
FLOGNY	Tuning fork	E.F.
FLORIET	Foil engraver's point	E.F.
FOLLIOT (CH)	Salt shaker	FOLLIOT
FONSEQUE ET OLIVE	Olive and branch	F.O.
FONTANA (CH)	Artistic fountain	C.F. et C.
FOTENEAU ET DUBOIS	Lance	F.D.
FORGELOT (ALBERT)	Portable forge	A.F.
FOUCART (LOUIS)	Hunting horn	L.F.

Name	Description of Mark	Initials or Words Appearing on Mark
FOUGERY (HENRI)	Chiseler's hammer	H.F.
FOUILHOUX (ED)	Ring dove	E.F.
FOUQUET (GEORGES)	Whip	G.F.
FOUQUET-LAPAR (G)	Goldsmith's chisel	G.F.L.
FOUQUETIERE (GEORGES)	Dog's head	G.F.
FOURNIER (VICTOR)	Small bird	V.F.
FOUROT (EDOUARD)	Scabbard	E.F.
FOVET (VVE)	Trowel	V.F. et C.
FOY (RENE)	Chisel and hammer of sculptor	R.F.
FRANCOIS (AUG)	Rabbit	A.F.
FRANCOIS (HENRI)	Bush	H.F.
FRANCOIS (LEON)	Heart in middle	L.F.
FRANCOIS (RAOUL)	Nasturtium	R.F.
FRECHOU (B)	Anchor	B.F.
FREMONT (ADOLPHE)	Pheasant	A.F.
FREREBEAU (LOUIS)	Key	L.F.
FREY (PAUL)	A swallow	P.F.
FRIBOURG	Femur bone	G.F.
FRION (G)	Dolphin	G.F.
FROIDEFON (GUSTAVE)	Vest tie	FROIDEFON
FROMENT-MEURICE (V)	Blade of wheat	F.M.
FRONTIN (ADOLPHE)	Two stars (one above, one below)	FRONTIN
GABERT (HENRI)	Large basket	H.G.
GABRIEL (HENRI)	Angel head	H.G.
GAGNEUR ET COMBET	Lizard	G.C.
GAILLARD (LUCIEN)	Notched pavillion	L.G.
GALAND (E)	Acorn with leaf	E.G.
GALLI (PIERRE)	A hen	P.G.
GARDET (JEAN)	Etcher's needle	J.G.
GARIOD (LEON)	Horn	L.G
GARMIGNY (EUGENE)	Oak leaf	E.G.
GARNIER (SIMON)	Game bag with three beads	S.G.
GAUDIBERT (JULES)	Waffle iron	J.G.
GAUTHIER (MARTIAL)	Five-pointed star, Greek cross on either side	M.G.
GAUTIER (G)	Rosette with six leaves	G.G.
GAUTIER (VVE A.)	Two poles crossed	A.G.
GAVAUDAN (EUG)	Three dashes or parallel lines	E.G.

Name	Description of Mark	Initials or Words Appearing on Mark
GELLE (CONSTANT)	Mirror	C.G.
GELLER (MEYER)	Crescent	M.G.
GENIN (JEAN)	Cat's head	J.G.
GENTELOT (EMILE)	Purse fastener	E.G.
GENTY (EDMOND)	Hand-mirror	E.G.
GEOFFROY	Star	F.G.
GEORGEON (ADOLPHE)	Horseshoe	A.G.
GERARD (ALFRED)	Four-leaf clover with star in center	A.G.
GERARD (AUGUSTE)	Weather and vane	A.G.
GERARD (VICTOR)	Two hammers crossed	V.G.
GERMAIN (GEORGES)	Hand	G.G.
GERMAIN (JOESPH)	Open hand	J.G.
GEROK ET CHARNAY	Nose	G. et C.
GIART ET GRISART	Torpedo boat	G. et G.
GIBERT (CH)	Mustard spoon with star	C.V.G.
GIBLET (CHARLEMAGNE)	Boat	C.G.
GIF ET FILS	Stock (flower)	G. et F.
GILBERT (HIPP)	A shell enclosing initials	H.G.
GILLE (EUG)	Bunch of grapes	E.G.
GILLES (ALBERT)	Bugle	A.G.
GILLES (VICTOR)	Drum	V.G.
GILLET (CH)	Cuff links	C.G.
GILLET (HENRI)	Vest	H.G.
GIRARDEAU (AUG)	Lighthouse	A.G.
GIRARDOT (B)	Mercury's bonnet	B.G.
GIRARDOT PERE ET POLET	Open fan	G.P.
GIRAUD (LOUIS)	Open knife	L.G.
GIROD (CH)	Glasses	C.G.
GIROUX (L)	Two stars with dash	L.G.
GODET (E)	Two maces crosswise	A.G.
GODIN (PAUL)	Small lamp	P.G.
GODIN (CHARLES)	C above, bowl below, name in middle	GODIN
GODIVIER (PAUL)	Etcher's needle	P.G.
GOLAUDIN (EUG)	*A*, English	E.G.
GOLDENSON ET LAURIE	Palm	G.L.
GOMBERT (ALPHONSE)	Standing lion	A.G.

Name	Description of Mark	Initials or Words Appearing on Mark
GOOSSENS (L)	A gondola	L.G.
GOUMANT (GUSTAVE)	Poodle	G.G.
GOUNEAUD (JULES)	Star	J.G.
GOURDON (ALFRED)	Blade of wheat	A.G.
GOUREAU (CELINI)	Palm tree	C.G.
GOVERNORE (VVE)	Rudder	G.C.
GRAILLOT (LEON)	Footed glass	L.G.
GRAND (A)	Mountain	A.G.
GRANDJEAN (ALEX)	Swallow with bead under head	A.G.
GRANVIGNE (G)	Vine stock	J.G.
GRATIANO (ISIDORE)	Cupid with arrow	I.G.
GRAVELIN (GEORGES)	Handle in form of crutch	G.G.
GRELLIER (FRANCOIS)	Grid	F.G.
GREMY (ALEXANDRE)	Music note	A.G.
GRENET (PAUL)	Beehive	P.G.
GRENIER (LEON)	Flying horse	L.G.
GRIGNON (LEON)	Piece of crust	L.G.
GRILLET (EDOUARD)	Two concentric circles	E.G.
GRIMPERELLE (GEORGES)	A small bird	G.G.
GRISEL (JEAN)	Cricket head to right	J.G.
GRIVEAU (LUCIEN)	Head of greyhound with star above and below	L.G
GROSS (ARMAND)	A winged wheel	ARMAND CROSS
GROSS (AUG)	Driver's whip	A.G.
GRUHIER (CECILE)	Crane	C.G.
GRUHIER PERE ET FILS	Piece of gruyere cheese	I.G.
GUERCHET (M)	Crozier	M.G.
GUERIN (CHARLES)	Stayed hands of watch	C.G.
GUERRE (CHARLES)	Royal staff	C.G.
GUEYTON (CAMILLE)	Winged anchor	C.G.
GUIBERT (CELESTINE)	Trident	C.G.
GUICHOT (VVE E)	Mistletoe	E.G.
GUILBERT (E)	Bodkin	E.G.
GUILLAUME (E)	Eagle with two heads	E.G.
GUILLEMIN FRERES	Holy Spirit above, heart below	G. FRES.
GUILLOT (GEORGES)	Vat	G.G.
GUILLON (PAUL)	Hunting rifle	P.G.
GUTPERLE	Helmet	R.G.

Name	Description of Mark	Initials or Words Appearing on Mark
GUTTIN (LOUIS)	Double gallons	L.G.
GUY (A)	Two branches of mistletoe crossed	A.G.
HAEK ET HOURDEQUIN	Two axes crosswise with star above	H et H
HAGE (HENRI)	Two axes in form of cross with a bead at each angle	H.H.
HAGNEAUX (ALBERT)	Lamb	A.H.
HAINSSELIN (F)	Winged foot	F.H.
HAMEL (A)	Gothic *H* with four stars, one on each side	A.H.
HAMET (ALP)	Hammer with crown	A.H.
HARDELLET ET MOUTON	A string bean, bead below	H et Cie
HARLEUX (CH)	Quarter of circle and hammer	HARLEUX
HARNICHARD (GEORGES)	Chariot	G.H.
HART (GEORGES)	Heart	G.H.
HATON (FRANCOIS)	June bug	F.H.
HEBERT (HENRI)	Hen	H.H.
HECTOR (A)	Star	A.H.
HEINZELMANN ET PASSEBOIS	Two wedding rings intertwined with *Cie* in the middle	H.P. H. FRERES
HELLER FRERES	Cow	E.H.
HEMERY (ED)	Sailboat	H. Cie
HENIN ET CIE	Rosebud and star below	C.H.
HENNIG (CH)	Anchor	A.H.
HENOCH (ARTHUR)	Sword	A.H.
HERBET (ALEXANDRE)	Branch of coral	D.H.
HERLIN (DESIRE)	Pole-axe	A.H.
HERRENKNECHT (ANDRE)	White skunk	A.H.
HERSANT (ALFRED)	Harrow or herse	E.H.
HIRTZ (EUGENE)	Head of hippopotamus	A.H.
HODEN (ALEX)	Crescent with star above	D.H.
HODIEUX	Head of Christ	J.H.
HOEL (JOURDAIN)	Lorgnette called monode	J.H.
HOFFMAN (JOS)	Open hand	J.H.
HOILER (JULES)	Sailboat with *R* in middle	L.H.
HOLLENDERSKI	Boat	A.H.
HOUDAN (ARM)	Hen on etcher's needle	T.H.
HOUILLIOT (TOUSSAINT)	A spit turner	J.H.
HUBERT (JEAN)	Double-faced axe	

Name	Description of Mark	Initials or Words Appearing on Mark
HUBERT (L)	Cameo	L.H.
HUIGNARD (EMILE)	Axe with handle	E.H.
HUREZ	Apple pierced by a sword	E.P.
HUVE (HENRI)	Two hands intertwined	H.H.
HYVELIN-LEPRINCE	A fish in oval	H. Le P.
JACHNOVITCH (OSIP)	Lion	O.J.
JACQUEMIN (HONORE)	Hand	H.J.
JACQUET (EMILE)	Jacket	E.J.
JACTA (GEORGES)	Paver's girl	G.J.
JAMOT (LEON)	Steering wheel	L.J.
JARRE (JEAN)	Jar	J.J.
JEAN (LEON)	Piglet	L.J.
JEKEL (STAN)	D above, E below	S.J.
JOBART FRERES	Glasses	J. FRES.
JOUANDON JEUNE (AMABLE)	Breton hat	A.J.
JOUANNET (D)	Horseshoe	D.J.
JOUSSET (MAURICE)	Strawberry	M.J.
JOUY FRERES	Tower	J. FRERES
JOZON (L)	Scythe	L.J.
JUSSY (ALF)	Circular saw blade	A.J.
JUSTE (ERNEST)	Jerkin	E.J.
KADZIK (EMILE)	Pipe	E.K.
KAEPPLER	Saturn	KAEPPLER
KAHN	Lathe	J.K.
KAHN ET CIE	Cross of Geneva and a star	K et Cie
KAMPER ET FUSIER	Kettle	L.K.
KATZ (VICTOR)	A vice	V.K.
KELLER (A)	Turtle	A.K.
KELLER FRERES	Head of Mercury winged	G.K.
KHAIN (FRANCOIS)	Anchor	F.K.
KINTZ (CH)	Ninepin	C.K.
KISCHINENSKY (SIMON)	Pliers	S.K.
KLAAS (LEON)	Two beads	L.K.
KOLB (JEAN)	Shirt collar	J.K.
KOVEN (EMM)	E above and a star beneath	KOVEN
KRONFELD (MAURICE)	Crescent	M.K.
LABAT (FRANCOIS)	Shoemaker's awl	F.L.
LABBE	Engraver's booth, star on sleeve	F.L.

Name	Description of Mark	Initials or Words Appearing on Mark
LABBE (ANTOINE)	Bell	A.L.
LABBOLLE (E)	Musical note La and a bowl	E.L.
LABOURIAU (CHARLES)	Camel	C.L.
LABRY (FELIX)	Open umbrella	F.L.
LACAZE (JULIEN)	House	J.L.
LACROIX (AUG)	Cross	A.L.
LAFARGUE (GEORGES)	Key	G.L.
LAFAYE (EDOUARD)	Three stars	E.L.
LAFFITTE (GASTON)	Palette crossed by crayon	G.L.
LAFORGE (ALF)	Clover and awl	A.L.
LAGRAVIER (E)	Creole crescent in filigree	E.L.
LAGRIFFOUL ET LAVAL	Three stars in a triangle	L.L.
LAHURE (AUGUSTIN)	Boar	A.L.
LALIQUE (RENE)	Sword	R.L.
LAMBERT (FRANCOIS)	Four-leaf clover with star above	F.L.
LAMBERT (JULES)	Medallion	J.L.
LAMBER (LEON)	Two oars in form of cross	L.L.
LAMBINET (FRANCOIS)	Hoe	F.L.
LAMBERT (ALBERT)	Retort	A.L. et S.
LANCON (EM)	Three lances in fan shape below the word	LANCON
LANDEAU (AMELIE)	Carriage	A.L.
LANDRY (L)	A spoon with a star in the bowl	L.L.
LANGLOIS (E)	Domino (Two double)	E.L.
LANGLOIS (EMILE)	Glove	E.L.
LANGLOIS (LUCIEN)	Bell	L.L.
LANGLOIS ET CHARTIER	Syringe	E.L.
LANGLOIS ET TIPHAINE	Frog	L. et T.
LANQUEST (EMILE)	Profile head of ram with star above	F.L.
LAPEYRE (GEORGES)	Clothes iron	G.L.
LAPEYRE (HENRI)	A spoon between two crescents	H.L.
LAPORTE (LEON)	Two wings	L.L.
LAPPARRA (ANTOINE)	Rat	A.L.
LAROCHE (AUG)	Hen	A.L.
LAROCHE (GUSTAVE)	Forget-me-not	G.L.
LATARASE (ADOLPHE)	General's hat	A.L.
LAUG (THEOP)	Palette	T.L.

Name	Description of Mark	Initials or Words Appearing on Mark
LAUNAY ET PETIT	*T.D.* intertwined	L.P.
LAURENT (MAURICE)	Laurel leaf	M.L.
LAURENT-POINTAUD	Screen	L.P.
LAUVAND (VINCENT)	A tulip surmounted by a wheel	V.L.
LAVANTURE (PROSPER)	Lyre	P.L.
LAVAULT (EDOUARD)	Music clef	E.L.
LAZARD (PAUL)	Lizard	P.L.
LECAPON ET AUBERT	Ant	L.A.
LECLERE (HENRI)	Lion's claw	H.L.
LECLERE (PHILLIPPE)	Lightning	P.L.
LECLEREQ (OSCAR)	Signet ring form, *O* with *L* below	O.L.
LECOEUR (EDOUARD)	Heart	E.L.
LEDENTU (H)	Tooth	H.L.
LEDERMANN (JOSEPH)	Star	J.L.
LE DOUBLE (FREDERIC)	Double *E* and double *L*	F.L.
LEDOUX (FELIX)	Two crosses back to back	F.L.
LEFEBVRE FILS AINE	Laurel stick	L.F.A.
LEFEBVRE ET PICARD	Two axes crossed	L.P.
LEFEVRE (AUG)	Pansy	A.L.
LEFEVRE (AOUL)	Carnation	R.L.
LEFORT (ALBERT)	Tower	A.L.
LEFORT-FRERES	Elephant's tooth	L. FRERES
LEGRAND (JEAN)	Bee	J.L.
LE JOLY NERAND ET CRENON	Four-leaf clover	N.J.N.C.
LELIEVRE (ACHILLE)	A standard, a star above	A.L.
LEMAITRE	Grenade with four flames	E.L.
LEMOINE	Cross of honor, a crown with three rosettes	V.L.
LEMOINE (ALEXANDRE)	Monk's head	A.L.
LENEUF (V)	Sugar tongs	V.L.
LEONHARDT (AUG)	Etcher's needle	A.L.
LEONNET	Two dolphins drinking from a bowl with word doubled	A.L.
LEPAGE (EUGENE)	Page's beret	E.L.
LEROY (ACHILLE)	A foot	A.L.
LEROY (AUG)	A lark on a rock	A.L.
LE SACHE	Candle ring	L.S.
LESAGE (ED)	Whip	E.L.

Name	Description of Mark	Initials or Words Appearing on Mark
LESAGE (ED)	Carrier	E.L.
LESPART (ADRIEN)	Arms of the city of Lesparre	A.L.
LEVY (EDOUARD)	A screw	E.L.
LEVY (J)	Ladder	J.L.
L'HERONDEAU (JEAN)	A swallow	J.L.
LHOMME (L)	A man with a round hat	L.L.
LHOTE (EDMOND)	Branch of mistletoe	E.L.
LIBKIND (MARCEL)	Crossed ring	M.L.
LIFSCHITZ (KALMAN)	Compass	K.L.
LIMOUSIN (ADELSAN)	Mason's trowel	A.L.
LINER (NAPOLEAN)	French hat	N.L.
LINZELER (ROBERT)	Royal crown	R.L.
LINZELER FRERES	A fish, bird over and under	E.L.
LITTEL (ANTOINE)	Astrakhan bonnet	A.L.
LOEB (LAZARE)	A star above	L. LOEB
LOLIERON ET DUPUIS	Booth	L.D.
LOMBARD ET LEVERT	Daisy	L.L.
LORET FILS	Parrot	L. ET FILS
LOSA (PAUL)	Head of lion	P.L.
LOWY (JOSEPH)	A scale	J.L.
LUNETEAU	A crescent and a vice	D.L.
LUNETEAU	Jerusalem cross	L.L.
LAQUIN (A)	Two nails	A.L.
MACAIRE (HENRI)	Four-leaf clover	H.M.
MACHERAT (L)	An axe	L.M.
MACLOS (GAB)	A star above	G. MACLOS
MAGNEN (AUG)	Etruscan vase	A.M.
MAGY (LOUIS)	Magic lantern	L.M.
MAILLARD FRERES ET JULES VAZOU	Goldsmith's mallet	M.V.
MAILLOT	A watch surmounted	M.
MAILLOT (LEON)	Number *1000* over number *100*	L.M.
MAINGOT (CAMILLE)	Open hand	C.M.
MAISON (LEON)	A small house	L.M.
MALEZIEUX	Mustard pot	V.M.
MALIN (EUGENE)	Greyhound	E.M.
MANCHUETTE	Chiseler's hammer	V.M.
MANDONNET (LOUIS)	Pitchfork	L.M.
MANGEOT (EMILE)	Cross of Lorraine	E.M.
MANGIN (LEON)	A helmet with two crayons across	L.M.

Name	Description of Mark	Initials or Words Appearing on Mark
MANGON (P)	Laurel crown	P.M.
MANTEAU (THEODORE)	Coat	MANTEAU
MANTOUX ET ROTTEMBOURG	Compass	M.R.
MANUFACTURE FRANCAISE	Pencil and pen holder	M.F.
MARAINES (SAMUEL)	Head of lion	S.M.
MARAIS (EMILE)	A mast	E.M.
MARC (CH)	Inkwell that cannot overturn	C.M.
MARCANT (LOUIS)	Chiseler's hammer	L.M.
MARCEAU (F)	Bucket	F.M.
MARCHAND (ETIENNE)	Steps	E.M.
MARCHAND (EUGENE)	Pig	E.M.
MARCHAND (MAURICE)	Man walking	M.M.
MARCOUS (G)	Runner	G.M.
MAREST (J)	Closed hand, index open	J.M.
MAREY (CHARLES)	Dash under letters	C.M.A.
MARIE (CH)	3/4 view of dog collar	C.M.
MARIE (ERNEST)	Thistle	AD.H.
MARIE (JULES)	Lighthouse	J.M.
MARIN-CUDRAZ	Mast with Latin sail	C.M.
MARMORAT FRERES	Medallion between two squares, engraver's point and rhombus	M. FRERES
MARMUSE (GUSTAVE)	A muse in a pool	G.M.
MARQUE (A)	Boat	A.M.
MARQUES (JOSEPH)	Compass, open star in middle	J.M.
MARRET FRERES	Three beads above and three beads below	M. FRES
MARSEILLE (CH)	Boat	C.M.
MARTIN (VICTOR)	A dry pear	V.M.
MARTINCOURT (HENRI)	Bishop's mitre	H.M.
MARTINCOURT (HENRI)	Table knife	H. MARTINCOURT
MASCHES (EDMOND)	Dutch galley	E.M.
MATHERET (PROSPER)	Caulking chisel	P.M.
MATHIEU (LEON)	Star	L.M.
MATRAT (LEONARD)	Palm	L.M.
MAUBUISSON (FRANCOIS)	Bush	F.M.
MAUCHAUSSE (ERNEST)	Man's shoe	E.M.
MAUGER (RAOUL)	Letter X	R.M.
MAURICE (PIERRE)	Fuse	P.M.

Name	Description of Mark	Initials or Words Appearing on Mark
MAY (B)	Rose	B.M.
MAZOYER BALME ET CIE	Clover	B. et Cie
MEIER-GRAEFE (JEAN)	Modern house above	L.M. et N.
MELINE (CH)	Cock	C.M.
MELLERIO (M)	Globe of world, point below	M.M.
MELLERIO-BORGNIS	Beehive	MELLERIO-BORGNIS
MELLES (J)	Crucifix and bird	J.M.
MEMBRE (ERNEST)	Muscle	E.M.
MENDEL (HENRI)	Antique vase	H.M.
MENETRIER (ADOLPHE)	Violin	A.M.
MENU ET FILS	Star	A.M.
MERCIER (PHILEAS)	A saw	P.M.
MERLE (CHARLES)	Tea strainer woven	C.M.
MERLIN (ALFRED)	Axe	A.M.
MERMILLOD (EUG)	Pavillion with star	E.M.
MESLET (F)	Rabbit's foot	F.M.
MESTIVIER (MARCEL)	Roman lamp	M.M.
MESTORINO (A)	Tower	A.M.
MEUNIER (LUCIEN)	Windmill	L.M.
MIANT (E)	Heart inflamed	E.M.
MICHAUT (V)	Two French marshall's batons in form of cross	V.M.
MICHEL	Propeller boat	E.M.
MICHEL (FERDUBARD)	Two hammers in form of cross	F.M.
MICHELIN (VICTOR)	Chalice	V.M.
MILARET (CESAIRE)	Cat	C.M.
MILLE (LEON)	Double star	L.M.
DILLER (DAVID)	Crescent	D.M.
MILLET (AMEDEE)	A clay key	A.M.
MILLET (HENRI)	A blade of millet grass	H.M.
MILLIARY (CH)	Anchor	C.M.
MIZIER (L)	Small lamp	L.M.
MOCHE (J)	Handful of silk	J.M.
MOCQUET (EUG)	Bucket	E.M.
MOLLARD (A)	Dolphin	A.M.
MOLLE (ED)	Dover	E.MOLLE
MOLLET (EUGENE)	Oyster bearing a pearl	E.M.
MOLLIET-CLAUDET (PHILLIPPE)	Spur	P.M.
MONDOLOT (JUST)	Scale	J.M.

Name	Description of Mark	Initials or Words Appearing on Mark
MONNEY (JULES)	Cup	J.M.
MOREAU (LOUIS)	Coin, star above and crescent below	L.M.
MOREL	An ear and decoration	M.F. et Cie.
MOREL (AUGUSTE)	Sheep standing on all fours	A.M.
MOREL (RENE)	A gear wheel	R.M.
MORGAN (EDGAR)	Walnut	E.M.
MORICAULT (CH)	Two stars	C.M.
MORIN (PAUL)	Four-pointed fork	E.M.
MORIN, FILLIOT, RICOIS ET CIE	Russian eagle	M.F.R. et CIE
MORIONDO (LOUIS)	Ox head	L.M.
MOSGAU (FRANCOIS)	Sailboat	F.M.
MOURET (EMILE)	Daisy	E.M.
MOUSSANI-STORA	A level	M.S.
MOUSSIE (CELESTE)	Hand vice	C.M.
MOUTON	Four-panel door	P.D.
MOUTON (GUSTAVE)	Sheep	G.M.
MOY (LEON)	Goose	L.M.
MURAT	Blackberry with two leaves and word doubled	C.M.
MURAT (CHARLES)	Blackberry with two leaves	C.M.
MUSSEL (HENRI)	Riveting hammer	H.M.
NATTAN (M EMILE)	A stork between initials	E.N.
NAU (YAHN ROBERT)	Cross with a star above	R.N.Y.
NEVEU (RENE)	Unmounted cannon	R.N.
NEY (VICTOR)	Two stars below	V. NEY
NIAUX (JULES)	Saint's niche	J.N.
NICOLINI	Necktie	O.N.
NICOT (ED)	Six-pointed star	E.L.F.N.
NIVELON (V)	Hook of an earring	J.N.
NOCQ (HENRI)	Crescent with two stars	H.N.
NOIREAU (J)	Two blacknotes separated by a star	J.N.
NORMAND (JULES)	Norman bonnet	J.N.
NOOSE (CH)	Key	C.N.
NUSBAUM ET HEROLD	Walnut with walnut leaf	N.H.
NUSBAUMER (ROBERT)	Upset heart	R.N.
OAFTI (H)	Hammer	H.O.
OBLATT (RODOLPHE)	A scale with columns	R.O.

Name	Description of Mark	Initials or Words Appearing on Mark
OKERMANS, POIRECUITE, ALEPEE ET CIE	A torch with three branches	S. et L.
OLIVE (VVE ESPERANCE)	Two stars below	VVE OLIVE
ORFEI (AUG)	Dancer	A.O.
ORTION (LUCIEN)	Two stars, one above and one below	L.O.
OSOUF	Religious cross	J.B. et V.P.
OSSELIN (CELESTIN)	Daisy	C.O.
PAGE (PAUL)	A page of impressions	P.P.
PAGET AINE	Serpent	A.P.
PAIN (VVE)	Two palms crosswise	VVE.P.
PAPOT (LEON)	Hat	L.P.
PARINI (A)	Foot	A.P.
PARIS (EDOUARD)	Key	E.P.
PARIS (LEON)	Chain	L.P.
PARMENTIER (A)	Potato	A.P.
PARTURIER (VVE MARILIS)	Sword	M.P.
PASTEYER (JOSEPH)	Comet	J.P.
PATIN	Skates	H.P.
PATTUSI (LAURENT)	Key	L.P.
PECONNET (CHARLES)	A pike surmounted by star	C.P.
PEGURET ET L. MONET	Bell	P.M.
PELLETIER ET CAVEND	Decaliter with number 10	P.C.
PELLETIER ET POURREE	Door knocker	E.P.
PELLOUTIER (MAURICE)	Bee, star on each side	PELLOUTIER
PENNELLIER (A)	Pencil case	A.P.
PEPIN (PAUL)	Trident and two beads	P.P.
PERLIN (ISIDORE)	Russian helmet	I.P.
PERRETTE (AUGUSTE)	Parakeet	A.P.
PERROT (JOS)	Hammer in form of cross	J.P.
PERSIANINOFF (ALEXIS)	Bear	A.P.
PERSINET (CH)	Crescent	C.P.
PETCHINOUK (LOUIS)	Bunch of grapes	L.P.
PETIT ET CIE	A hand, star above	P.W.
PETRE (AMEDEE)	Cross of Lorraine	A.P.
PEYRE (ALB)	Razor	A.P.
PHILIP (JACOB)	A poor devil	J.P.
PHILIPPE (L)	Scale	L.P.
PIA (JULES)	Cross surmounted by a heart	J.P.
PIBLINGER (ALEXANDRE)	Pipe	A.P.

Name	Description of Mark	Initials or Words Appearing on Mark
PICARDAT (PHILIPPE)	Cross of Lorraine	P.P.
PICHARD (CH)	A sword and a pen crosswise	C.P.
PICOT (THEOPHILE)	A pike, a point above	T.P.
PICOT (VICTOR)	Pickaxe	V.P.
PICQ (HENRI)	Ace of spades	H.P.
PIEL (L)	Anchor, word doubled	L.P.
PIEL FRERES	Sword	P.FRERES
PIERRE (AUG)	Leaf	A.P.
PINARD (VVE)	Eel	VVE C.P.
PINAU (J)	Tweezers	J.P.
PLANCHE (MARC)	Wild duck	M.P.
PLANTADE (LOUIS)	Standing lion	L.P.
PLATON (ANTOINE)	Cornflower	A.P.
PLICHON (V)	Square and a rhombus	V.P.
PLISSON ET HARTZ	Cat seated	P.H.
POCHIET (ALP)	Bottle	A.P.
POINCELET (FELIX)	Sheaf	F.P.
POISSON (EDOUARD)	Swallow	E.P.
POISSON-DELPORTE	Fish	P.D.
POLAK (E)	Sword	E.P.
POLINGHI (GAETANO)	An eye	G.P.
POLLAK (SALOMON)	Snake	S.P.
PONCE (J)	Rattle with ring	P. FRES L.
PORLIER (HIPPOLYTE)	Ace of clubs	H.P.
POTHIER ET NAUDEZ	Two stars	P.N.
POTONNIER (EDMOND)	A bridge	E.P.
POUPAR (L)	Stock (flower)	L.P.
POURNOT (CLAUDE)	Dog	C.P.
POUSSIELGUE-RUSANDD ET FILS	A cross, an anchor, a heart, and a star	P.R.F.
POUZENQ (J)	Oak leaf with star above	J.P.
PREAUX (FERNAND)	Number 3 between letters	F.P.
PRETET FRERES	Tree	P. FRERES
PREVOST RECIPON ET CIE	Antique lamp	P.R. et CIE
PROT (EUG)	Two stars	E.P.
PRUDHOMME (EDMOND)	Heron crowned	E.P.
PRUDHOMME (ERNEST)	Caduceus	E.P.
PRUDHOMME (GEORGES)	A dragon	G.P.
PUIFORCAT ET TABOURET	Penknife	E.P.

Name	Description of Mark	Initials or Words Appearing on Mark
QUEILLE	Antique oar	P.Q.
QUERCIA (JANVIER)	Oak leaf	J.Q.
RACOVSKY FRERES	Rat, point each side	R. FRERES
RACOWSKY FRERES	Two sabres crossed as X	R. FRERES
RAGAULT (CHARLES)	Rat	C.R.
RAMBOUR (ANDRE)	Apple	A.R.
RAMBOUR (CH)	Poplar tree	C.R.
RASSE (GUSTAVE)	Half-open razor	G.R.
RAT (PAUL)	Chameleon	P.R.
RAVIENT (L)	Covering in form of cross	L.R.
RAVINET ET CH	Shaded clover surmounted by a star	R.D.
RAVINET D'ENFERT	A dove	R.D.
RAY (EMILE)	Three points of a triangle	E.R.
RAYAT (ALFRED)	Serpent	A.R.
REDDE (GEORGES)	Ear	G.R.
REGNIER (EMILE)	Hammer and spindle tree entwined	E.R.
REIGAGNE (FRANCOIS)	Chandelier	F.R.
REMY (J.M.)	Pitcher	M.R.
REMY (VALENTIN)	Musical notes D and E	V.R.
RENIMEL (P)	Reindeer	P.R.
RENN (FELIX)	Head of reindeer	F.R.
REZZAGHI (JOSEPH)	Anchor surmounted by star	J.R.
RIBBOT (MARIUS)	Horseshoe	M.R.
RICHSTAEDT (P)	Two rings entwined	H.R.
RIFFAUD (GEORGES)	Greyhound	G.R.
RINGEL (ERNEST)	Enameled ring in a star	O.R.
RIONDE (GEORGES)	Caduceus	G.R.
RIONDET (HENRI)	A star above	RIONDET
RISLER ET CARE	Star and square	R.C.
RIVAUD (CH)	Light battery	C.R.
RIVIERE (G)	Anchor	G.R.
RIVIERE (HENRI)	Small boat	H.R.
RIVIERE (THEODORE)	Faucet of fountain	T.R.
ROBIN (ALFRED)	Elder bush with three points above and three points below	A.R.
ROBIN (EMILE)	Cube	E.R.
ROBIN (PAUL)	Fan	P.R.
ROBINEAU (E)	Arrow, point down	E.R.

Name	Description of Mark	Initials or Words Appearing on Mark
ROCHAIN (THEOPHILE)	Faucet	T.R.
ROCHAS ET LAGRUE	G above and star below	ROCHAS
ROCHE FRERES	Rock	R. FRERES
ROCHER (JULES)	Squirrel seated	J.R.
ROCHERIEUX (JULES)	Magnifying glass and handle	J.R.
RODIER FILS	Wooden shoe	R. FILS
ROGER (AUG)	Buffoon	A.R.
ROGER (EUGENE)	Compass and hammer intertwined	E.R.
ROLLET ET APPERT	Japanese character	R. et A.
ROPITAUX (DENIS)	Re-Mi-Do (music notes)	D.R.
ROSSIGNOL (EM)	Lieutenant's cap	E.R.
ROTEMBERG (AD)	Alsatian head	A.R.
ROUBEROL (GEORGES)	Wheel and anchor	G.R.
ROUGELET ET DELATRE	Open alliance	R. et D.
ROUILLON (JEAN)	Crescent	J.R.
ROUSSEAU (BENJAMIN)	Spiral	B.R.
ROUSSEAU (JULES)	Bucket	J.R.
ROUSSEAU (PAUL)	Anchor	P.R.
ROUSSEL-DOUTRE	Domino (double two)	D.R.
ROUSSELLE FRERES, TIREIN ET CIE	Spinning wheel	R. FRES T ET C
ROUSSET FRERES	Bird	F.R.
ROUX (LOUIS)	Wheel imposed over booth	L.R.
ROUX (V LOUISE)	Wheel	L.R.
ROUX (CH)	Wheel with two wings in center	C.R.
ROUX (VVE JEANNE)	Coat of mail	VVE J.R.
ROZ (ERN)	Rose	E.R.
RUAULT (ADOLPHE)	A line	A.R.
RUAULT (LOUIS)	Watch pendant Louis XV	L.R.
RUFF (MAURICE)	Button screw	M.R.
RULANCE (ACHILLE)	Stream coming from rock	A.R.
RUTHENBURG (JULES)	Four-leaf clover	J.R.
SAGE (AUGUSTE)	Two stars above	A. SAGE
SAGLIER FRERES ET CIE	Anchor	S.F.
SAINSOT (ALPHONSE)	Five pails (two, two, and one)	A.S.
SAINT-MAXEN (EDOUARD)	Heart with star above	S.M.
SAINT-PAUL	A branch of lily entwined with a sword	ST-P.

Name	Description of Mark	Initials or Words Appearing on Mark
SAINT-YVES	A hammer and two etcher's needles	S.Y.
SALT ET SCHLOSBERG	Two swords in form of a cross with star above	S.S.
SAMETT (HENRI)	Sabre	H.S.
SAMSON (CHARLES)	Star above a cross	C.S.
SANCAN (JOSEPH)	Reappearance of a head	J.S.
SANDOZ (GUSTAVE)	Star	G.S.
SANGUIN (LEON)	Ring of watch	L.S.
SANIER (FRERES)	Basket with flowers	S. FRERES
SANNER (EMILE)	Tongue hanging out of lion's head	E.S.
SANTT (JULES)	Triangle with point in center	J.S.
SARRAZIN (P-F)	Blade of wheat	F.S.
SAUDINOT(FOIS)	Bucket	F.S.
SAULCE (JULIES)	Eye	J.S.
SAUSSET (G)	Alpenstock above and alpine rose	G.S.
SAVARD ET CIE	Crescent, two stars, and words	DOUBLE SAVARD
SAVARD ET CIE	Crescent, two stars, and word	A. SAVARD
SCAGLIA (CH)	Ox head	C.S.
SCHAEFER (OSCAR)	A cat and a flat iron	O.S.
SCHAEFFER (PAUL)	Four arrows in form of cross	P.S.
SCHETZ (L)	A star between two letters	L.S.
SCHIFFERLET (EUG)	Lyre	E.S.
SCHOULTZ (VVE)	Cardinal's epaulet	E.S.
SCOCZYNSKI (NICODEME)	Two hands intertwined	N.S.
SEJOURNE (HENRI)	Rose, star above	H.S.
SENECHAL (GEDEON)	A star with point above and below	G.S.
SENEN (NICHOLAS)	Tuft of rye grass	N.S.
SERBOURSE (GABRIEL)	Eagle's claw with a closed purse	G.S.
SERIEYS	Greyhound	E.S.
SERVIERES (JOSEPH)	Bird's head	J.S.
SESTACQ (GEORGES)	A beret with 6 below	G.S.
SEYSSAUD (AUG)	Treble clef	A.S.
SIERE (CHARLES)	Five-leaf clover	C.S.
SILVESTRE (FRED)	Pine	F.S.
SIMON (DENIS)	Crescent with two stars	SIMON

Name	Description of Mark	Initials or Words Appearing on Mark
SIMON (SLISONSKY)	A scalp	S.S.
SIMONOT (PAUL)	Twig off a vine	P.S.
SMETS (HENRI)	Tea spring	H.S.
SOCIETE ANONYME LA LUNETTERIE PARISIENNE	Cross, four points	L.P.
SOCIETE DES ALLIAGES DES METAUX	An anchor upside down with star below	S.A.M.
SOCIETE DES LUNETIERS	Candelabra with three brands	S.L.
SOLIE (A)	Domino (double six)	A.S.
SORMANI (PAUL)	Two stars	P.S.
SOUABE (ANDRE)	Ace of clubs	A.S.
SOUCHET ET CIE	Duck standing	S. ET CIE
SOUDAN (E)	A molar tooth with crescent below	E.S.
SOUFFLOT (HENRI)	Rising sun and star	H.S.
SOUFFLOT (PAUL)	Necktie	P.S.
SOULOY (LEON)	Shoe	L.S.
SOURIS (ALEXANDRE)	Mouse	A.S.
SOURY (LOUIS)	A star above and a star below	LOUIS SOURY
STEINER (ALBERT)	Large bell	A.S.
SUSSE (E)	Spigot	E.S.
TABARY	Bolt of door	E.T.
TALABOT (J-B)	Heart on fire	J.B.T.
TALLOIS (ALB)	Open umbrella with a star below	A.T.
TALLOIS (AM)	Iron crown with a point above	AM.TALLOIS
TALON (FELIX)	Star	F.T.
TARDANI (PIETRO)	Turtle	P.T.
TAROT (JULES)	Horseshoe	J.T.
TEMPLIER	A knight with hammer	C.T.
TEMPLIER (JOSEPH)	Facade of temple	J.T.
TESTART (ALBERT)	Tadpole	A.T.
TETARD (EDMOND)	A Huguenot woman	E.D.T.
TETARD (PHILIPPE)	Tadpole in an aureole	P.T.
TETERGER (H)	Woman's breast	H.T.
THEILHABER (CHARLES)	Wad-extractor	C.T.
THENAULT (MARC)	Barrel	M.T.
THIBAULT (ALBERT)	Flowerpot	A.T.
THIBAUT (ALEX)	Pear	A.T.

Name	Description of Mark	Initial or Words Appearing on Mark
THIBAUT (ALEXANDRE)	Shears	A.T.
THIBOUVILLE (EDMOND)	Corkscrew	E.T.
THIERRY (DE)	Star, two points above	M.T.
THIERRY (CHARLES)	Numeral 1 divided into three equal parts	C.T.
THOREL	Telegraph	D.T.
TILLESE (ISAAC)	Harp	I.T.
TIRBOUR (CHARLES)	Travelling bag	C.T.
TIXIER ET BEAUDET	Great bell	T.B.
TOUCHARD (ALB)	Heart pierced by dagger	A.T.
TOULOUT (GEORGES)	Wolf	G.T.
TOURNAN (LEON)	Turning lathe	L.T.
TOURNANT (JEAN)	Lamp	J.T.
TRANCHANT (ALFRED)	Bee	A.T.
TRAUS (PIE)	Tiara	P.T.
TRAUTMANN (MICHEL)	Three points	M.T.
TRELAT (ALPHONSE)	A club card	A.T.
TRIEBEL (JOSEPH)	Tripod	J.T.
TRIOULLIER	Cruet	T. et FILS
TROMBETTA (JOSEPH)	Trumpet	J.T.
TROUVE (EUG)	A fly in a crescent	E.T.
TURIN (JULES)	Rabbit running, a star above	J.T.
TURPIN (A)	Painter's palette	A.T.
UCCIANI (PIERRE)	A lion with tail upright	P.U.
VAGNIER (EDMOND)	Basket	E.V.
VAGUER (ALEXANDRE)	*A* above, home and star below	VAGUER
VAGUER (LEON)	Crescent	VAGUER
VALARCHER (THEODORE)	Bow of violin	T.V.
VALENTIN (ALFRED)	Star	A.V.
VANDERBELEN (P)	Small bellows	P.V.
VANDERHEYM (LEON)	Leaf of parsley	L.V.
VANDERHEYM ET DUMENIL	Steering wheel	V.R.
VANDEVOIR (JOSEPH)	Cat	J.V.
VANDROOGENBROECK (LEON)	Two stars	L.V.D.
VANHOOSTENRICK (VVE)	Elephant	VVE.V.
VANGUIN (HIPP)	A winnowing machine	H.V.
VAN MINDEN ET CIE	Dutch mill	V.M.
VAN NERUM	Vase with two handles	F.V.

Name	Description of Mark	Initials or Words Appearing on Mark
VASTOCK (GEORGES)	Parrot	G.V.
VAUMARIN (CAMILLE)	Seal	C.V.
VAUTTAVERS (FRED)	Cancer (sign of zodiac)	F.V.
VEDY (ALBERT)	Snail	A.V.
VEECK (GUILL)	Crossbow	G.V.
VEILLARD (ARMAND)	Night light	A.V.
VENNER (PIERRE)	Ladder	P.V.
VENOSTA (JEROME)	Hammer	J.V.
VENTRE (FRANCOIS)	Clover	F.V.
VERGER ET OUDIN	Footed glass	V et O.
VERGNON (JEAN)	A glass	J.V.
VEVER (E)	Anchor	E.V.
VEYRAT	One line between two stars plated	VEYRAT
VEYRAT	Two stars	A.V.
VEYRAT (GUST)	Footed glass	G.V.
VIAL-MILLERET	Chandelier with three lights	V.M.
VIALLET (LOUIS)	Spoonbill made of earrings	L.V.
VIANO (A)	Pig's head	A.V.
VIETTE (A)	Ostrich feather	A.V.
VIGNIER ET GALLOIS	Cross of St. Louis	V.G.
VILLAIN (LEON)	Ring of crucible	L.V.
VILLAUME (CH)	Chalice	C.V.
VINCENT (CHARLES)	2000 kg weight	C.V.
VINCENT (LEON)	*20/100*	L.V.
VINCENT (RAYMOND)	Die, two points	R.V.
VINCENT-GARCE (G)	Cross of the Legion of Honor	V.G.
VIRLEX (E)	A comma	E.V.
VITAL	A glassmaker's diamond	V.H.
VITTON (FERDINAND)	Seated dog	F.V.
VOISENET (HIPP)	Head of Mercury	H.V.
VUILLERET (PIERRE)	A double saltshaker	P.V.
VUILLERMOZ (LOUIS)	A crescent, star within	L.V.
WAGENHEIM (MAURICE)	Two lances in form of cross	M.W.
WAGNER (ALBERT)	The word *espoir* (hope)	A.W.
WALBERT ET V BURTIN	Chinese cage	W. et B.
WARME (LUCIEN)	A clover	L.W.
WEISSMANN (HENRI)	Scythe	H.W.
WIESE	A star above and one below	WIESE
WOLF ET MATHIS	Two pipes entwined	B.W.

Name	Description of Mark	Initials or Words Appearing on Mark
WOLLES (BENJAMIN)	Hunting horn	B.W.
YENCESSE (OVIDE)	Blade of wheat	O.Y.
YTASSE ET FOURNERET	Sheep	Y.F.
ZALKING (HENRI)	A scarab	H.Z.
ZEINER (CH)	Cap with two points above	C.Z.
ZIEGLER (EMILE)	Hammer	E.Z.
ZORRA (L)	Roman Eagle inside wreath	L.Z.
ZOUCKERMANN ET CIE	A star, crescent in center	Z. et CIE
ZWEIFELD ET COSTE	Pig	Z. et CIE

Other Jewelers Working In Art Nouveau Style In Paris Circa 1900

ALTENLOH, MAISON
ANDRE (AL)
AUGE ET VIAL
BEAUCLAIR (R)
BEAUGRAND
BECKER (E)
BELLEVILLE (E)
BING, MAISON (MARCEL)
BLONDAT (M)
BONNY (L)
BOTTE (L)
BOUCHER (L)
BOUTET DE MONVEL (CH)
BOUVET (R)
BRAILLARD (G)
BRATEAU (J)
BRUNEAU (A)
BUCHER (A)
CHADEILHAC, MAISON
CASAULTA, MAISON
COLONNA (E)
DEBULT (E)
DE RIBEAUCOURT (G)
DESBOISY (J)
DESCHAMPS (L)
DESROSIERS
DESCOMPS (JOE)
DE SUAU de LA CROIX (COMTE)
DUBRET (H)
DUFRENE (MAURICE)
FILINOIS-TROUILLE
FOLLOT (P)
GAUTRAIT (L)
GEROCH et CHANAY
GRASSET (E)
HAAS, MAISON
HAMELIN, MAISON
HAMM (H)
HEURTEBISE (L)
HIRNE
HIRTZ (L)
HOWLLON, MAISON
JONVIER (L)
LAMBERT (TH)
LEFEVRE (C)
LETURCO
MELLERIO, MAISON
MODERNE
PROUVE (V)
ROUZE, MAISON
ROZET (R)
RUFFE (L)
SAINT-IVES
SALLES (R)
THESMAR (⊞F)
THESMAR ET HERNE
TOURETTE (E)
ZORRA (L)

Medallists

DUPUIS
PATEY
ROTY
BOTTEE
LECHEVREL
DUPRE
COUDRAY
CHARPENTIER
CHAPLAIN
VERNON
VERNIER
PROUVE
YENCESSE
DELOYE
DREGOIRE
FUCHS
BOURGEOIS

English Jewelers Circa 1900

These marks are examples of those found on gold jewelry made in England. If the jewelry was imported to London after 1958, the mark *F* is stamped on it. In contrast to the practice in France, however, compliance with these marking regulations for jewelry has been very lax in England.

Standards of gold for jewelry produced in England are as follows:

Prior to 1854	22 carat
1854-1932	9, 12, 15 & 18 carat
After 1932	9 & 14 carat

22 K 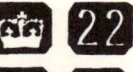   14 K

18 K    9 K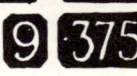

Prominent English Jewelers & Guilds of the Late 19th Century*

ARTIFICERS GUILD   Mark: *As. GD.L.D.* enclosed in a shield

The firm was founded in 1901 and its chief jewelers were Nelson Dawson, Edward Spencer, and J. P. Cooper.

ASHBEE, CHARLES (1863-1942)   Mark: *CRA GOH Ltd.*

Founded School and Guild of Handicraft (GOH Ltd.) in 1887, which dissolved in 1908. Ashbee influenced the Arts & Crafts movement as well as the jewelry of Dawson, Gaskin, Sampson, and Liberty & Company.

ASPREY & CO.   MARK: *Asprey & Co.*

Prominent commercial jeweler in London.

BIRMINGHAM GUILD OF HANDICRAFT   Mark: *GHoH* in a square

The chief jewelers were F. R. Gittins and H. R. Fowler.

CARR, ALWYN (1872-1940)   Mark: *Rn & Cr* in rectangular shield

Associated with Omar Ramsden.

CHILD & CHILD   Mark: Sunflower with *C C* on either side (Also, shield with *C C*)

Emphasized enameled silver jewelry in Arts & Crafts style, but also produced some fine enameled gold jewelry.

COOPER, J. PAUL (1869-1933)   Mark: *JPC* (in a shield)

Worked under Henry Wilson and produced Arts & Crafts style jewelry with singular enameling and often in gothic style. Also made Japanese type jewelry using copper and silver.

CUZNER, BERNARD (1877-1956)   Mark: *BC*

Probably designed jewelry for Liberty and the Birmingham Guild of Handicraft.

DAWSON, NELSON & EDITH   Mark: *ND* in an ivy leaf

Founded Artificers Guild and produced Arts & Crafts jewelry with delicate enamels, emphasizing birds and flowers.

---

*Note: For detailed English marks see *Old Silver*, by Seymour Wyler (New York: Crown Pub., 1937).

FISHER, ALEXANDER (1864–1936) Mark: *AF* (on the enamel)

Distinguished enamelist chiefly on copper and silver. Made only a small amount of jewelry, but his contribution to Arts & Crafts style and enameling was significant.

GARRARD, R. & S. Mark: Firm name

Outstanding jewelry firm in London specializing in precious stones.

GASKIN, ARTHUR Mark: *AJG*

Designed pieces of jewelry in Arts & Crafts style characterized by curling gold and silver wire, enriched with semi-precious stones.

GILBERT, SIR ALFRED (1851–1934)

Noted sculptor who designed only a few pieces of jewelry.

GUILD OF HANDICRAFT Mark: *G of H Ltd*

HANCOCKS & CO. Mark: Firm name

Made excellent precious stone jewelry and reverse crystal intaglios.

HART, DOROTHY

Produced slender and filigree pendants with enamels and pearls.

KING, JESSE (1876–1949) Mark: *Liberty & Co.*

Designed jewelry for Liberty & Co.

KNOX, ARCHIBALD (1864–1933) Mark: *AK*

Designed jewelry for Liberty & Co. in the "Cymric" style.

LIBERTY & CO. Mark (for Cymric line): *Ly & Co.* in a triple diamond

Fostered "Cymric" jewelry from 1899 and helped establish Arts & Crafts design and jewelry. Liberty designs and jewelry were made by leaders of the movement such as Knox, Gaskin, Cuzner, and Haseler.

MURPHY, H. G. (1884–1939) Mark: *HGM*

One of the best enamelers in jewelry in the Arts & Crafts and Art Deco style. He was influenced by Henry Wilson, but developed his own characteristic and distinctive enameling colors and style. His pieces are frequently signed and still can be purchased. Generally enameled the backs of his jewelry.

MURRLE, BENNETT & CO. Mark: *MB & Co.*

Produced large numbers of small jewelry in the Arts & Crafts style and also in the German style of Art Nouveau. Competitors of Liberty & Co. (although see chapter IX). There are comparatively few, if any, master pieces of jewelry that have been produced with their mark.

NEWMAN, MRS. PHILLIP (1870–1910) Mark: *MRs N* in a rectangle

Specialized in archeologic jewelry because she was associated with John Brogden. Her signed pieces can still be purchased and have become collector's items.

PARTRIDGE, FRED Mark: Partridge

Made Arts & Crafts jewelry but also produced some pieces in the French Art Nouveau style. Not many of his pieces are available commercially.

RAMSDEN, OMAR Mark: *Rn & Cr* in shield *Omar Ramsden me Fecit*

Produced many pieces of jewelry in Art Nouveau and Arts & Crafts styles, but employed many to produce the pieces.

RICKETTS, CHARLES (1866–1931)

RUNDELL, BRIDGE & CO.
Produced outstanding Victorian precious stone jewelry, but not in the style of Arts & Crafts.

SEDDING, G. E.   Mark: *GES*
Made Arts & Crafts jewelry mostly of silver and copper with semi-precious stones.

SIMPSON, EDGER   Mark: Name in circle
Produced jewelry in Arts & Crafts style for Artificers Guild. Was especially fond of colorful and iridescent enamels.

SPENCER, EDWARD (1872–1938)
Designed jewelry similar to Ashbee's exphasizing enameled silver with mother-of-pearl.

STABLER   Mark: *HS*
Designed and produced Arts & Crafts jewelry and English Art Deco.

WAINRIGHT, G. J.   Mark: Firm name
Produced enameled jewelry in Giuliano style and some Arts & Crafts style pieces.

WILSON, HENRY (1864–1934)   Mark: *HW* in monogram
Outstanding proponent of Arts & Crafts jewelry. Produced numerous important masterpieces. Excellent enamelist and jeweler.

WINTOUR, MARY
Used very rich and delicate enamels in Arts & Crafts style.

Other English Jewelers Circa 1900

ALABSTER, A.	FRAMPTON, G.	McNAIR, J.
ALLEN, K.	GEBHART, A.	NOUFFLARD, ANNIE
ANGUS, C.	GRAYHORN, A.C.	MILLS, E.
ARSCOTT, A.	HADWAY, W.S.	PHIPPS, MISS
AWDRY, M.	HAMMETT, L.	RANKILOR, G.
BAKER, O.	HODGKINSON, W.	PICKETT, E.
BARRIE, B.J.	HORTI, P.	SILVER, R.
BERGER, ARTHUR	JAHN, C.C.	TRAQUAIR, P.
BRANGWYN, F.	JONES, A.H.	VARLEY, F.C.
BROWN, E.M.	LAVEROCK, F.	VEAZEY, D.
BURGES, W.	MACDONALD, M.	VIRTUE, ETHEL
CONDOR, F.	MACKINTOSH, C. (SCOTLAND)	VIMER, E.
COOK, T.		VOYSEY, C.
DALE, L.G.	MACLISE, D.	WEST OF DUBLIN (IRELAND)
DAVIDSON, WILLIAM	MARK, W.	
DAY, LILY	MARTINEAU, M.	WHITE, W.W.
DROPSY, E.	McBEAN, I.	
EVER-SWINDELL, N.	McLEISH, M.	
FISHER, K.	McNAIR, F.	

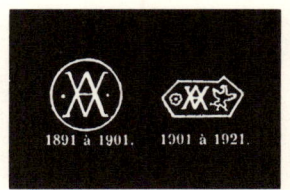

Austria

with imperial eagle to right, means imported to Austria 1901 - 1921.

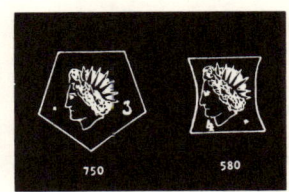

FISCHMEISTER, H.
GRINGOLD, E.
HAUPTMANN, F.

HOFSTETTER, J.

HOLZINGER, E.
MESMER, F.

NANTHE, G
PRUTSHER, O.
ROSET, H.
SCHWARTZ, PROF.
WAGNER, ANNA
UNGER, E.

Belgium

CASSIERS, H.
DuBOIS, P.
HOOSEMANS, F.
POMPE, L.

ROMBAUX, E.
VANSTRYDONK, L.
WOLFERS, P.

Denmark

BOLLIN, M.
BUNDESBOLL, TH.
JENSON, G.

MAGNUSSEN, E.
SLOTT-MOLLER, H.

Germany

ARNOLD, J.	MAYER, V.
BASTIANER, G.	MOHRING, B.
BECK, O.	MORAWE, C.
BISSINGER, C.	MULLER, C. W.
CRANACH, W. L.	NIENHAUS, L.
EIBERGER, J.	OLBRICH, J.
FAHRNER, TH.	OTT, H.
FIESSLER, L.	RIESTER, E.
GOSEN, T.	RINGER, A.
HIRZEL, H.	SCHILLING, E.
KLEEMAN, G.	SPROSSLER, A.
KOCH, R.	ULLRICH, W.
KOHLER, P.	WERNER, L.
KOPP, E.	ZERRENNER, (FIRM)
LOWENTHAL, D.	

Holland

EISENLOEFFEL, J.	HOEKER
HOCKETET, FILS	NIEUWENHAUS

Russia

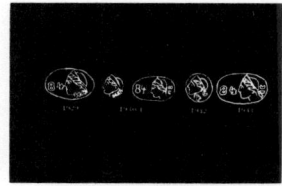 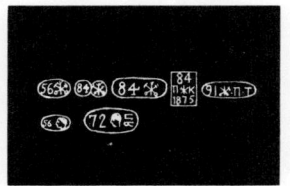

BEILIN	SAZYKOV
BOCK	IVAN SALTYKOV
BOLIN	I. OZERITSKI
BRITZIN	GREGORY SBITNEV
BUTZ	MISHUKOV
DENISSON	J. VASILEV
GRATCHOV	ANTON KUZMICHEV
RIMMER	OREST KURLIUKOV
KARL HAHN	NICHOLAI ALEKSEEV
NICHOLS AND PLINKE	VASILII AGAFANOV
	MARIA SEMENOVA
OVCHINNIKOV	I. ROKKOMOVSKI
IVAN KHLEBNIKOV	

THE ARTELS FOR EXAMPLE IS 3Я△ THIRD ARTEL

FABERGÉ WORKMASTERS (NOT ALL MADE JEWELRY)

E.K.—ERIK KOLLIN
M.П.—MICHAEL PERCHIN
H.W.—HENREK WIGSTROM
I.P.—JULIUS RAPPAPORT
A.H.—AUGUST HOLMSTROM
A.T.—ALFRED THIELEMANN
A.H.—AUGUST HOLMING
B.A.—VIKTOR AARNE
A.A.—HJALMAR ARMFELT
A.N.—ANDERS NEVALAINEN
G.N.—GABRIEL NIUKKANEN
T.R.—PHILIP RINGE

B.C.—VLADIMIR SOLOVIEV
A.M.—ANDERS MICHELSON
—G. LUNDELL
Ф.A.—FEDOR AFANASSIEV
E.S.—EDWARD SCHRAMM
W.R.—WILHEIM REIMER
A.J.—ANDREJ GORIANOV
S.W.—STEPHAN WAKEVA
O.P.—OSKAR PIHL
Ф.P.—FEDOR RUCKERT
A.P.—ALEXANDER PETROV
Ф.P.—FEDOR RAUCH

POSSIBLE FABERGÉ EMPLOYEES

N.П.
E.W.
I.C.A.
A.R.
П.А.
А.Б.

В.Ф.
Ж.С.
Ф.Н.
С.В.
А.В.
Л.N.

The Leningrad Jewelry Brotherhood took over Fabergé premises and completed some of the unfinished Fabergé pieces. They stamped their own mark on these pieces.

ЛЮТ

Spain and Portugal

CASHIRA-Y-CARRERAS

MASRIERA, L.

Switzerland

BECKER, E.

GOLAY FILS

Bibliography

Amaya, M. *Art Nouveau*. London, 1966.

———. "Liberty and the Modern Style." *Apollo*, vol. 77 (1963), p. 109.

Ames, W. *Prince Albert and Victorian Taste*. London, 1968.

Armstrong, Nancy. *Jewellery, an Historical Survey of British Styles and Jewels*. London, 1973

Ashbee, C. R. *Modern English Silverwork*. Essex House Press, 1909.

———. "A Short History of the Guild and School of Handicraft." *Transactions of the Guild and School of Handicraft*, vol. 1 (1890), pp. 19-31.

Bainbridge, H. C. *Peter Carl Fabergé*. London and New York, 1949.

———. *Peter Carl Fabergé*. London: Spring Books, 1966.

Banister, Judith. *Collector's Guide*. London, 1970.

Bapst, G. *Histoire des Joyaux de la Couronne de la France*. Paris, 1889.

Becker, Vivienne. *Antique and 20th Century Jewelry*. London: N. A. G. Press, 1980.

Bénédite, L. "Lalique." *Revue de l'Art Décoratif*, July 1900.

———. "Les Salons de 1898." *Gazette des Beaux-Arts*, June 1898.

Billcliffe, R. "J. H. Macnair in Glasgow and Liverpool." Liverpool: Walker Art Gallery, *Annual Report and Bulletin*, vol. 1 (1970-71).

Bing, S. *La Culture Artistique en Amerique*. Paris, 1896.

Black, J. A. *A History of Jewelry*. London: Orbis Pub., 1981.

Blakemore, K., ed. *The Retail Jeweller's Guide*. London, 1973. (Includes a section on hallmarks with facsimiles).

Bloche, A. *La Vente des Diamantes de la Couronne*. Paris, 1888.

Bott, G. *Kunsthandwerk, um 1900*. Darmstadt: Edward Roether Verlag, 1965.

Bott, G., and Citroen, K. *Jugendstil*. Sammlung K.A. Citroen. Darmstadt: Hessiches Landesmuseum, 1962.

Bradford, E. *English Victorian Jewellery*. London, 1959.

———. *Four Centuries of European Jewelry*. Country Life, Ltd., 1953.

British Museum. *The Jewelers Art*. Edited by H. Tait and C. Gere. London: British Museum Pub. Ltd., 1978.

———. *Jewelry Through 7000 Years*. London: British Museum Pub. Ltd., 1976.

Brunhammer, Y., et al. *Art Nouveau: Belgium, France*. Houston, Tex.: Rice University, 1976.

Bulgari, C. C. *Argentieri, Gemmari e Orafi d'Italia*. Rome, 1958.

Burty, P. *F.D. Froment-Meurice, Argentier de la ville de Paris*. Paris, 1883.

Bury, Shirley. "A Liberty Metalwork Experiment." *Architectural Review*, 1963.

———. "An Arts and Crafts Experiment, the Silverwork of C. R. Ashbee." *Victoria and Albert Museum Bulletin*, vol. III, no. 1 (January 1967), p. 18.

———. *Jewellery Gallery, Summary Catalogue*. London: Victoria and Albert Museum, 1982.

———. "Pugin's Marriage Jewellery." *Victoria Albert Museum Yearbook*, 1969.

Carré, L. *A Guide to Old French Plate*. New York: Charles Scribner and Sons, 1931.

Castellani, A. *Della Oreficeria Italiana*. Rome, 1859.

———. *Antique Jewellery and its Revival*. London, 1861.

Cleveland Museum of Art. *Japonisme*. Kent State University Press, 1975.

Clifford, Anne. *Cut-Steel and Berlin Iron Jewellery*. Bath, England, 1971.

Colonna, E. *Essay on Broom Corn*. Dayton, Ohio: Privately printed 1887.

Connaissance Bijoux Etonnants, pp 56-65. Paris: Ferrier, 1964.

Curran, Mona. *Collecting Antique Jewelry*. New York: Emerson Books, Inc., 1963.

Curtis, C. Densmore. *Jewelry and Gold Work*. Rome: Sindacato Italiano Arti Grafiche, 1925.

Darling, Ada. "American Victorian Jewelry." *American Collector*, vol. 12 (November 1943), pp. 10–11.

Davenport, Cyril. *Cameos*. London, 1900.

———. *Little Books on Art Jewellery*. London, 1905.

de Kay, C. *The Art Work of Louis C. Tiffany*. New York: Privately printed, 1917.

d'Otrange, M. L. "The Exquisite Art of Carol Giuliano." *Apollo*, vol. 59 (1954), pp. 145–152.

Dumont, F. "Froment-Meurice, le Victor Hugo de l'Orfèvrerie." *Connaissance des Arts*, vol. 57 (1956).

Evans, Joan. *A History of Jewellery, 100-1870*. London and New York, 1923. Rev. ed. London, 1970. (Contains very extensive bibliography).

Falkiner, R. *Investing in Antique Jewelry, 1968*. New York: Clarkson N. Potter Books.

Ferriera, Maria T. G. "René Lalique at the Calouste Gulbenkian Museum, Lisbon." *Connoisseur*, vol. 177, no. 174 (1971), pp 241–249.

Flower, Margaret. *Victorian Jewellery*. London and New York, 1951. Rev. ed. London, 1967.

Forbes, Christopher. *Fabergé Eggs*. New York: Abrams, 1980.

Forrer, L. *A Biographical Dictionary of Medallists*. London, 1919.

Fouquet, G. *Bijouterie, Joaillerie, Medailles à l'Exposition Internationale de Milan, 1906*. Paris, 1913.

Fouquet, Jean. *Bijoux et Orfèvrerie*. Paris: Charles Moreau, 1928.

Frank, Joan. *The Beauty of Jewelry*. New York: Crown Pub., 1979.

Fregnac, Claude. *Jewelry from Renaissance to Art Nouveau*. New York: G. P. Putnam's and Sons, 1965.

Gazette des Beaux Art, 1898-1900.

Gere, Charlotte. *Victorian Jewellery Design*. London, 1972.

———. *American and European Jewelry, 1830-1914*. New York: Crown Pub., 1975.

Gilbert, Ruth. "American Jewelry from the Gold Rush to Art Nouveau." *Art in America*, vol. LIII, no. 6 (1965-66), p. 80.

Goldenberg, R. L. *Antique Jewelry*. New York: Crown Pub., 1976.

Grigorietti, G. *Jewellery Through the Ages*. London and New York, 1970.

Heydt, G. F. *Charles F. Tiffany and the House of Tiffany and Co*. Privately printed for Tiffany and Co., 1893.

Hinks, P. *19th Century Jewelry*. London: Faber & Faber, 1975.

Hoffman, J., ed. *Der Modern Stil*. Annual vols. 1897-1916, Stuttgart.

Holme, C., ed. *Modern Design in Jewellery and Fans*. Studio special number, 1901-02.

———, ed. *Arts & Crafts*. London, Paris, New York: Studio, 1916.

Honour, H. *Goldsmiths and Silversmiths*. London, 1971.

Horta, Victor. *Le Bijou 1900*. Brussels, May 1965.

Hughes, G. *The Art of Jewelry*. London, 1972.

———. *Modern Jewelry*. London, 1963.

———. *Modern Silver*. London, 1970.

Janson, Dora. *From Slave to Siren*. Chapel Hill, N.C.: Duke Museum of Art, 1972

Koch, Robert. *Louis C. Tiffany, Rebel in Glass*. New York, 1964.

Kris, E. *Catalogue of the Post-Classical Cameos in the Milton Weil Collection.* Vienna, 1932.

Lalique, Marc. *Lalique par Lalique.* Paris: Société Lalique, 1977.

_____. Personal Communication, 1965.

Laurvik, J. N. *René Lalique.* New York, 1912.

Lewis, M. D. S. *Antique Paste Jewellery.* London, 1970.

Madsen, S. T. *Art Nouveau.* London, 1967.

Marks of the Jewelers and Kindred Trades, USA, 1900-1906. Radnor, Pa.: Jewelers Circular Pub. Co., Jewelers Circular Keystone.

Massim, O. "Lucien Falize, Orfèvre, Joaillier." *Gazette des Beaux Arts,* 1897, p. 343.

Meusnier, G. *La Joaillerie Francaise en 1900.* Paris, 1901.

Museum of Modern Art. *Art Nouveau.* New York: Doubleday and Co., 1960.

Naylor, Gillian. *The Arts and Crafts Movement.* London, 1971.

Newark Museum. "Silver in Newark." *Newark Museum Bulletin,* 1966.

L'Orfèvrerie La Joaillerie. Paris: Editions du Chene, 1942.

Peter, Mary. *Collecting Victorian Jewellery.* London, 1970.

Les Poincons de Garantie. Paris: Tardy, 1975.

Poincons de Maître, 1899-1902. (M. Morin, Dir.) Privately printed. Paris.

Rainwater, Dorothy. *American Silver Manufacturers (Facsimilies of marks and trademarks).* Hanover, Penn., 1966.

_____. *American Silver Manufacturers.* New York: Crown Pub., 1976.

Reade, B. *Alphonse Mucha and Art Nouveau.* H.M.S.O. for the Victoria and Albert Museum. London, 1964.

Review Bijouterie, Joaillerie, Orfèvrerie. Paris, 1900-1904.

Rhiems, M. *L'Objet 1900 Arts et Meitiers Graphiques.* Paris.

Roche, J. C. *The History, Development and Organization of the Birmingham Jewellery and Allied Trades.* Suppl. to Dial., 1927.

Ross, M. C. *Fabergé and his Contemporaries.* Cleveland Museum of Art, 1965.

Sataloff, J. "Belle Epoque Baubles." *19th Century,* vol. IV, no. 2 (1978).

Sataloff, J., and Richards, A. *Jewelry and Gemstones.* London: Octypus, 1975.

Scheffler, W. *Werke Um 1900.* Berlin: Kunst Museum, 1966.

Shurr, G. "Berlin: A Study of the Art of 1900." *The Connoisseur* (American Edition), September 1966, p. 44.

Schmutzler, R. *Art Nouveau.* New York, 1962.

Selz, P., and Constantine, M. *Art Nouveau.* New York Museum of Modern Art, 1959.

Smith, H. C. *Jewellery.* London and New York, 1908. Reprint. London, 1973.

Snowman, A. K. *Carl Fabergé, Goldsmith to the Imperial Court of Russia.* London: Debrett, 1979.

_____. *The Art of Fabergé.* London, 1953.

Steingraber, E. *Antique Jewellery, 800-1900.* London, 1957.

Sutherland, C. H. V. *Gold.* London, 1959.

Twining, Lord. *A History of the Crown Jewels of Europe.* London, 1960.

Vever, H. *La Bijouterie Francaise au XIX Siècle.* Paris, 1904-08.

von Hapsburg, George, and Solodkoff, Alexander. *Fabergé.* London and New York: Christie's and Studio Vista, 1979.

Walters Art Gallery. *Jewelry, Ancient to Modern.* New York: Viking Press, 1976.

Wartski. *A Thousand Years of Enamel.* London, 1971.

Wilson, Henry. *Silverwork & Jewelry.* London: Putman & Co., 1978.

Waterfield, Hermione, and Forbes, Christopher. *Fabergé: Emperial Eggs and Other Fankines.* New York: Scribner's, 1978. (Recently reprinted by Clarkson N. Potter Books).

Woodhouse, C. P. *Victorian Collector's Handbook.* London, 1971.